HOW CITIES WORK

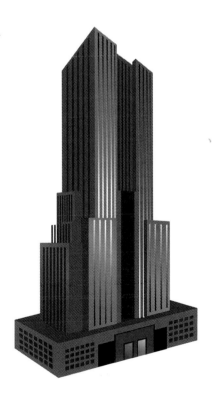

HOW CITIES WORK

PRESTON GRALLA

Illustrated by
DAVE FEASEY AND MINA REIMER

Ziff-Davis Press
Emeryville, California

Development Editors	Mary Johnson and Kelly Green
Technical Reviewer	Natalie Macris
Project Coordinator	Cort Day
Proofreader	Nicole Clausing
Cover Copywriter	Valerie Haynes Perry
Cover Illustration and Design	Regan Honda
Book Design	Carrie English
Technical Illustration	Dave Feasey and Mina Reimer
Word Processing	Howard Blechman
Page Layout	M.D. Barrera and Joe Schneider
Indexer	Anne Leach

Ziff-Davis Press books are produced on a Macintosh computer system with the following applications: FrameMaker®, Microsoft® Word, QuarkXPress®, Adobe Illustrator®, Adobe Photoshop®, Adobe Streamline™, MacLink®*Plus*, Aldus® FreeHand™, Collage Plus™.

For information about U.S. rights and permissions, contact Chantal Tucker at Ziff-Davis Publishing, fax 212-503-5420.

If you have comments or questions or would like to receive a free catalog, call or write:
Ziff-Davis Press
5903 Christie Avenue
Emeryville, CA 94608
800-688-0448

ISBN 1-56276-324-5

Manufactured in the United States of America
10 9 8 7 6 5 4 3 2 1

As always, for Lydia, Mia
and Gabriel.

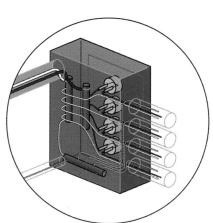

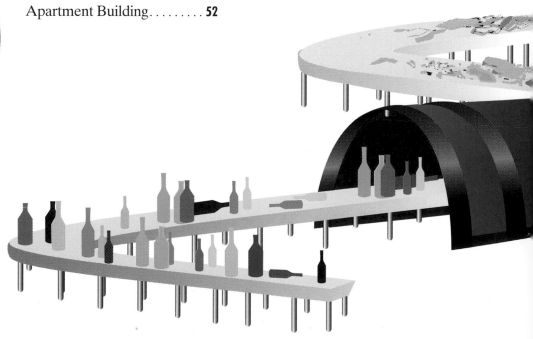

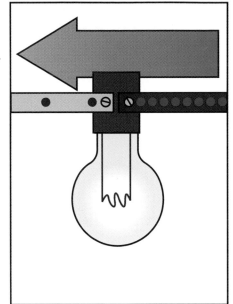

PART 3

Going Up: Construction in the Cities
91

PART 4

Moving Machines: Transportation in the City
111

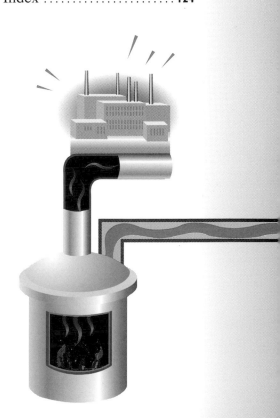

This book wouldn't have been possible without the help of many people. Thanks go to Robert Healy, City Manager of Cambridge, Massachusetts, for giving me a remarkable overview of how virtually every aspect of a city works, from plowing the snow to delivering the water to cleaning the streets. He also gave me full run of the City of Cambridge's many departments. Steve White, Cambridge's Assistant Commissioner of Public Works, was a great help as well. Assistant Commissioner White is a veritable poet of pipes; he explained to me in vivid and exquisite detail the remarkable workings of the pipes, conduits, and lines just beneath our feet. I'll never look at a public construction site again with quite the same set of eyes, thanks to him.

Several books were of aid as well. *The City in History,* by Lewis Mumford, published by Harcourt, Brace, and World, was tremendously helpful to my own understanding of the origin and cultural transformations of cities throughout time. Also of vital importance was the remarkable book, *A Scientist in the City,* by James S. Trefil, published by Doubleday, which explained much about the scientific and ecological concepts underlying the technology and natural world of today's city.

The book also wouldn't be possible without the aid of everyone at Ziff-Davis Press. Thanks to Cindy Hudson for believing in the book; Cheryl Holzaepfel, for making sure that it would work; and development editors Mary Johnson and Kelly Green and project coordinator Cort Day, for helping with organization, shepherding the book through its creation, and making my writing sound better than it should. Thanks too, should be given to Dave Feasey and Mina Reimer for the illustrations, Howard Blechman for word processing, M.D. Barrera and Joe Schneider for page layout, Nicole Clausing for proofreading, and Regan Honda for the cover.

And, of course, I'd like to thank my wife Lydia and my children Gabriel and Mia. They've put up in good faith with my maundering about conduits, pipes, and concrete for too long.

Utilities: The Urban Environment's Hidden World

CONTENTS

D ON'T LOOK NOW, but beneath your feet there's a hidden world. It's a world that sizzles with electricity, that's inundated with water, that smolders with steam. It's a world that sees millions of cubic feet of natural gas stream by, that carries telephone and computer communications and television signals. It's a world that brings untold millions of gallons of fresh water and takes away millions of gallons of water-borne waste.

When you walk city streets, you see a great deal of life around you, but the truth is, there's as much activity beneath the city as there is above it. And without this hidden underground life, without thousands of miles of cables and lines and pipes and wires, life above ground would be impossible.

Utility lines and cables snake around each other in labyrinthine ways; there are complex financial relationships among the companies that own and run these utility lines. Electric, telephone, and cable TV lines, for example, generally are run through pipes called conduits, which are clustered and sunk in concrete. These conduits have room for more than one set of lines, so the telephone, electric, and cable TV companies at times share them, and pay one another for renting the space inside.

In Part 1 of this book, we'll look at some remarkable, often unseen journeys: water that travels hundreds of miles underground, natural gas that is sent thousands of miles through underground pipes, and electricity that travels hundreds or thousands of miles as well, at nearly the speed of light.

In Chapter 1, we'll focus on an overview of all the pipes and lines beneath the city streets. Through cutaway views, we'll see how all these pipes and lines fit together. We'll see which ones are built closest to the surface and which ones are sunk deepest. And we'll look at the entranceways to the city's hidden world—the manholes that are ever-present in our city.

Chapter 2 examines what may be the most precious and often overlooked natural resource of all—fresh water. Millions of gallons of water makes its way from distant reservoirs to houses and office buildings in the city. Along the way, the water is routed through a complex series of pipes, is cleaned at a treatment plant, and then snakes in underground pipes through city streets before it magically appears whenever you want it from your tap.

In Chapter 3, we'll look at what may well be the twentieth century's crowning technological achievement, but one that we take for granted—electricity. We'll start at the source, at a power plant—in this case a coal-powered electricity-generating plant—and we'll see how electricity is generated. Then we'll see how that electricity is routed through the power grid to your home. And finally, we'll see exactly how that power runs through the wires in your home and affects every aspect of your life.

Chapter 4 details a more ancient source of light and power—the gas system. Gas has been used for nearly 3,000 years, and to a great degree, the way it is routed has not changed in a millennium. It is taken from its source then channeled through pipes so that it can be used elsewhere. We'll see how the millions of cubic feet of gas make their way from distant gasfields to modern cities.

Chapter 5 looks at a part of the city that most of us don't care to think about very much—sewer systems and garbage collection. It's far from an unsavory subject, however, because in some ways, these systems are the most important of all. While medical technology has certainly lengthened our lifespans, modern sanitation has saved many lives as well. Because of it, we are no longer subject to the plagues and waterborne disease that ravaged civilization in the past and that continue to ravage some parts of our world today. In this chapter we'll also look at how we are trying to stop polluting the earth—by recycling vast amounts of paper, plastic, glass, and other materials.

Chapter 6 examines a technology that is of the future as much as today—communications technology. When you hear of the much-vaunted "information superhighway," this is what they're talking about—the wires and cables strung overhead or buried beneath the streets. Telephone and cable television, while they seem rather mundane and even somewhat old-fashioned by now, are in fact the infrastructure upon which the twenty-first century communications revolution will be built—and we'll take a look at how it all works.

All these wires and cables and conduits and pipes may be interesting, but they're really only important because of what they provide to us—the services they bring directly into our homes. And so in Chapter 7, the final chapter in this part, we'll see how it all comes together. We'll look at a cutaway view of an apartment building and see how and why our buildings stand up. And we'll look inside the walls and see how the utilities and services are brought directly to us.

So get a pair of your virtual x-ray glasses ready, because we're about to go on a tour of the hidden world. After you visit, you may never look at the city in the same way again.

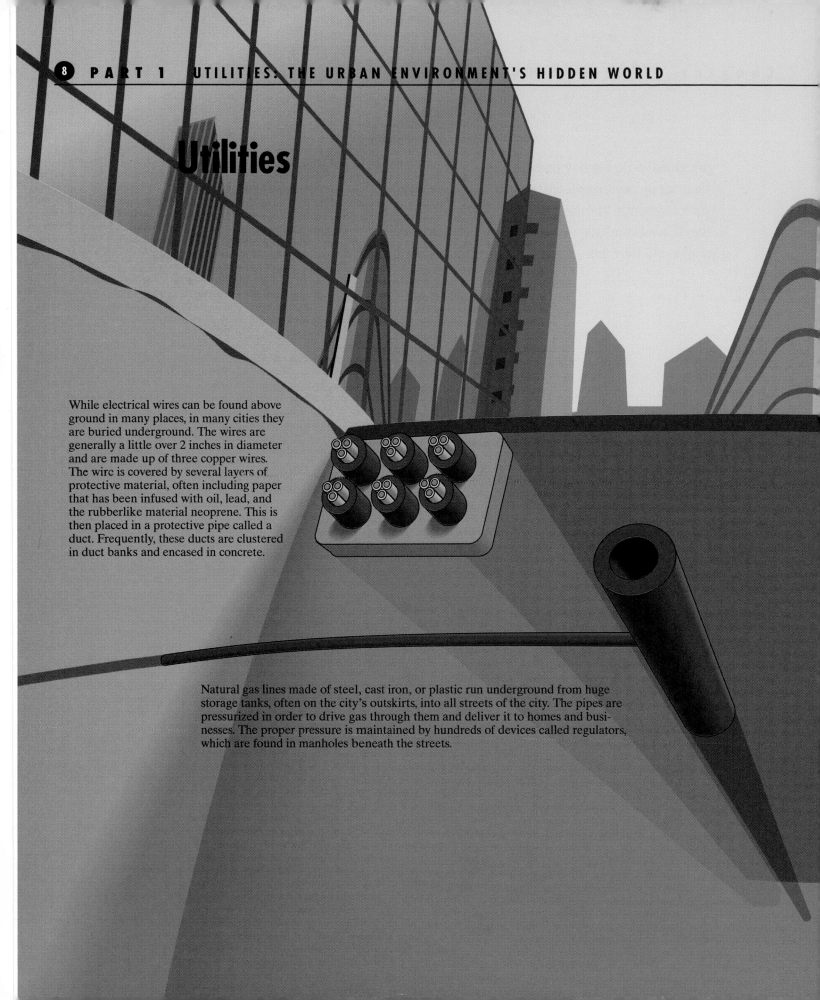

Utilities

While electrical wires can be found above ground in many places, in many cities they are buried underground. The wires are generally a little over 2 inches in diameter and are made up of three copper wires. The wirc is covered by several layers of protective material, often including paper that has been infused with oil, lead, and the rubberlike material neoprene. This is then placed in a protective pipe called a duct. Frequently, these ducts are clustered in duct banks and encased in concrete.

Natural gas lines made of steel, cast iron, or plastic run underground from huge storage tanks, often on the city's outskirts, into all streets of the city. The pipes are pressurized in order to drive gas through them and deliver it to homes and businesses. The proper pressure is maintained by hundreds of devices called regulators, which are found in manholes beneath the streets.

All utility lines throughout the city—whether they be electrical, steam, or sewage—require regular maintenance. Workers access these lines through manholes. Each system has its own distinctive manholes into which workers can descend or else can lower tools and other devices in order to maintain the system. A telephone manhole is pictured here.

Telephone wires, like electrical wires, can be located above or below ground. They are bound together in cables about 3 inches in diameter and then encased in rubberlike neoprene. These cables are then protected by ducts and bound in clusters by concrete. More modern telephone lines use fiber-optic cable instead of copper cable. In addition to allowing for much higher-speed communications, a single fiber-optic wire can carry many more calls than copper can.

In some cities, electric companies don't merely deliver electricity to buildings—they also furnish steam, which is used for heating. Originally, this steam was shipped from electricity-generating plants, since it was a byproduct of the process of generating electricity. As demands for steam grew, and as the technology of electricity-generating plants altered, complete power plants were built to generate steam. Mains—which can be 2 feet in diameter—carry steam from the plant to points in the city; submains then carry steam down individual streets; and service pipes carry the steam into individual buildings. Since steam pipes are hot, and could damage other utility lines, they are buried deep, at least 6 feet underground, and are encased in concrete.

Water and Sewer Lines

Each component of the city's life support system has its own place in the hidden world just beneath city streets. Ideally, closest to the surface—often a scant 2 feet below it—are the electrical and telephone wires. Heavy utilities—water and gas pipes—are on the next level down. Steam pipes are lower still—at least 6 feet underground—because of the heat they generate. Frequently, at the lowest level of pipes is the storm drain and sewer system.

To deliver water throughout the city from reservoirs or storage tanks, water is pumped through underground pipes. Low-pressure pipes deliver water to the city's houses, stores, and industries, while higher-pressure lines are frequently used for fire hydrants. The largest pipes, called mains, are built of concrete, steel, or cast iron and carry water from pumping stations to distribution points throughout the city. Smaller submains branch off from the mains and deliver water to every street in the city. Branch lines, the smallest pipes in the water-delivery system, branch off from mains and bring water to every building in the city.

In many ways, the sewage system is a mirror of the water system. Pipes carry sewage from individual buildings into larger lateral pipes. These laterals then flow into even larger submains. Several submains flow into still-larger mains, and all the mains in turn empty into a single, huge pipe called the interceptor, which carries the sewage into a sewage treatment plant, where it is cleaned and purified.

Storm drains empty water that accumulates in city streets from storms and from other sources. Other fluids, such as oil and grease from cars, also find their way into the storm drain system. Because storm drains have to be capable of carrying away—in a short time—massive amounts of water from heavy rains, their pipes are much larger than sewer pipes—often ten times the size. They are frequently located beneath all the other pipes in the city. In some cities, storm drains are combined with the sewage system, often causing significant pollution of waterways. In heavy rainstorms, so much water flows through the combined system that treatment plants sometimes can't keep up with the volume and discharge untreated sewage directly into waterways.

How a Water Treatment Plant Works

1 Most cities get their water from large reservoirs, which can be located near the city or in some cases hundreds of miles away. In order to cut down on pollution of the reservoir, cities often purchase sizable watersheds around it and don't allow the watersheds to be used for industry, commerce, or recreation. Water is sent to the city from the reservoir through a series of dams and pipes. It flows via gravity and may also require a series of pumps.

2 Before water from the reservoir can be used, it must be treated, disinfected, and cleaned of pollutants in a water treatment plant. The intake pipes extending from the reservoir to a treatment plant usually have a series of grates and screens that keep out fish, logs, and other large objects.

Lime

Alum

3 Frequently, the water contains suspended matter—organic materials that allow bacteria to grow, and minerals that can give the water a bad taste. Chemicals—notably aluminum sulfate, also known as alum—are added to the water to remove this suspended matter. The alum clings to the matter in the water, causing it to congeal into large particles of floc. This entire process is known as coagulation and flocculation. Lime is sometimes added to the water to remove minerals. Water with a high percentage of minerals is called "hard" water; adding lime "softens" it.

Sedimentation tank

4 The water and floc flow into a sedimentation tank or basin. The floc settles to the bottom of the tank, where it is removed.

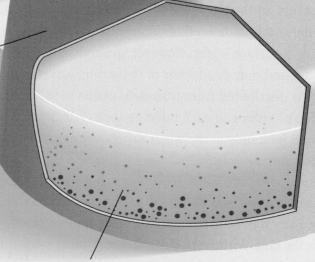

Floc

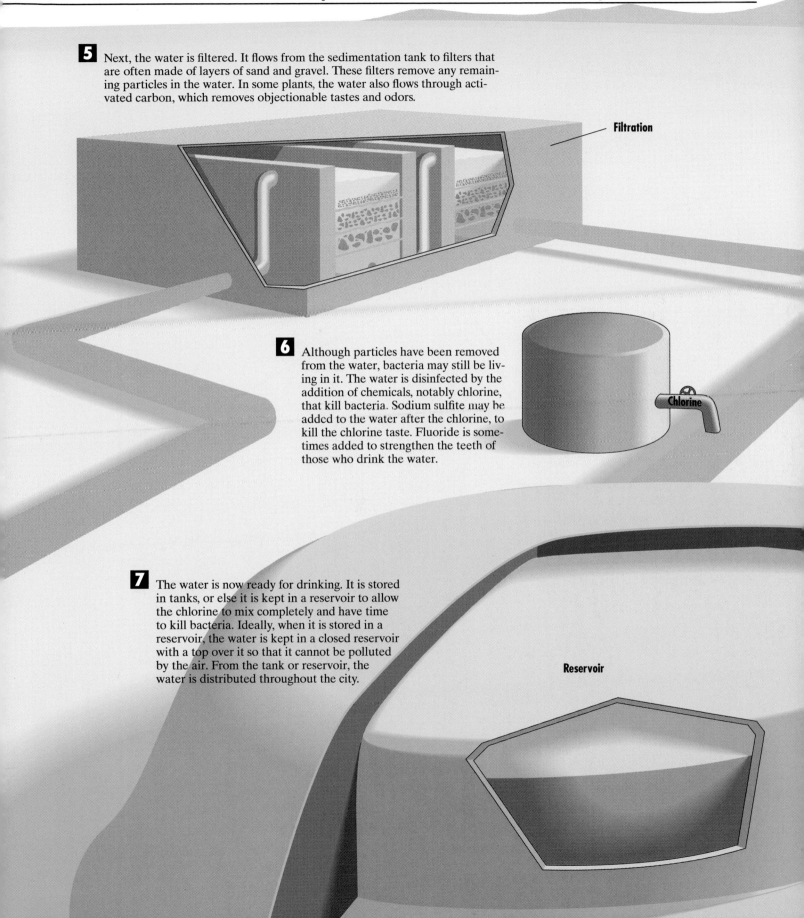

5 Next, the water is filtered. It flows from the sedimentation tank to filters that are often made of layers of sand and gravel. These filters remove any remaining particles in the water. In some plants, the water also flows through activated carbon, which removes objectionable tastes and odors.

Filtration

6 Although particles have been removed from the water, bacteria may still be living in it. The water is disinfected by the addition of chemicals, notably chlorine, that kill bacteria. Sodium sulfite may be added to the water after the chlorine, to kill the chlorine taste. Fluoride is sometimes added to strengthen the teeth of those who drink the water.

Chlorine

7 The water is now ready for drinking. It is stored in tanks, or else it is kept in a reservoir to allow the chlorine to mix completely and have time to kill bacteria. Ideally, when it is stored in a reservoir, the water is kept in a closed reservoir with a top over it so that it cannot be polluted by the air. From the tank or reservoir, the water is distributed throughout the city.

Reservoir

Water tank

How Water Is Delivered

1 After water is purified at a treatment plant and stored in a closed tank or reservoir, it is ready to be delivered throughout the city via the water system. In some areas, the water is first pumped into tall storage tanks. In order for the water system to work properly, a constant pressure must be maintained so that water flows into homes and other buildings. Having water in storage tanks helps maintain the pressure since the force of gravity pushes water from the tanks into distribution pipes. Pumps at pumping stations are also used to maintain the pressure.

2 From storage tanks, the water flows through mains, which are made up of cast iron, concrete, clay, or steel. The mains flow from pumping stations or storage tanks into every part of the city.

Fire hydrant

Main

7 Some cities maintain a separate water system for fire prevention. This water system operates at a higher pressure than the drinking system and supplies water to the fire hydrants. Fire hoses need high pressure water from hydrants so that they can pour large amounts of water into buildings in a short time in order to put out fires.

Submain

Branch line

Valve

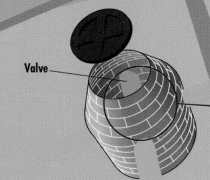

3 Smaller pipes, called submains, branch off from the mains and travel down every street in the city. Branch lines, even smaller than the submains, branch off of submains and bring water from the submains into individual buildings.

4 When a pipe in the water system requires repair or replacement, there must be a way to shut off water to just that pipe without disrupting water service throughout the city. This is done by valves inside the pipes, which can be lowered to stop the flow of water. Valves are located on all branch lines so that water can be easily cut off to individual buildings. Valves are also located at distances of several hundred feet along mains and submains.

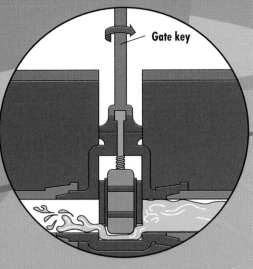

Gate key

Manhole

5 To close a valve, a long-handled device called a gate key is first lowered through a *valve box*—a small hole in the street with a square or round iron lid on it, a familiar sight on many city streets. The gate key turns a nut on top of the valve, which in turn lowers the valve through the pipe and cuts off the water supply.

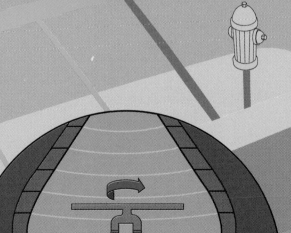

6 Some valves are so large they can't be turned by using a gate key. In these cases, the valve is found in a manhole beneath the street, topped by a manhole cover, which, when opened, allows a person to climb into the manhole and turn the valve. Typically, manholes for the water system are built of curved concrete or bricks and are several feet deeper than a person is tall.

How Water Flows through Your Home

1 The branch line that brings water into a building is buried deep enough underground so that it doesn't freeze in the winter. A main shut-off valve at the point where the line enters the building allows all water to be shut off if the plumbing system in the building needs repairs.

2 The water pressure maintained by the city's water distribution system is generally powerful enough to force the water to the first five or so stories of a building. Buildings taller than that need an internal pump to circulate the water. The pump may direct water throughout the building or, instead, into a storage tank on the roof. From this tank, the pressure of gravity allows for distribution of water throughout the building.

3 At the point where the branch line enters the builders, smaller pipes branch off and carry some water to a hot water heater, usually powered by gas or electricity. The rest of the water is carried in cold water pipes. Hot water and cold water pipes circulate through the entire building. Older pipes are made of lead or cast iron, while newer ones are galvanized steel. Lead pipes were used by the Romans two thousand years ago—in fact, the word *plumbing* comes from the Latin word for lead, *plumbum*. Lead pipes—and copper pipes soldered with lead—may be a health hazard because lead can be leached out of them and into drinking water. Modern pipes are built out of copper or plastic.

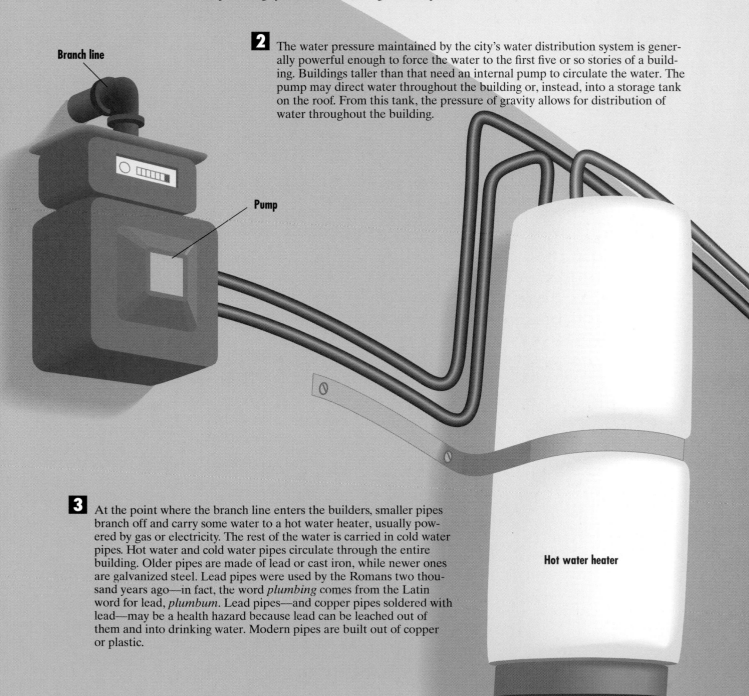

Branch line

Pump

Hot water heater

4 A *screw tap* is one of two common types of faucets used in a home. A screw tap controls either the hot or the cold water, but not both at the same time. When the handle is turned, it moves a spindle, or screw, which in turn raises a rubber washer. When this rubber washer is raised, water flows through the tap. When the screw is turned in the opposite direction, the washer is lowered, and the water is cut off.

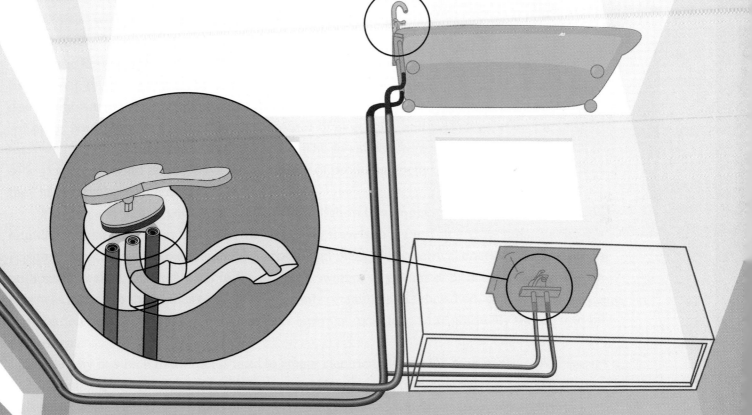

5 A mixing tap, the other type of faucet, controls both hot and cold water pipes at the same time. A lever moves a piston, which, when turned in different directions, mixes hot and cold water from the pipes in various proportions.

How a Coal-Fired Power Plant Works

1 The burning of fossil fuels—coal, oil, and natural gas—accounts for approximately 70 percent of all electricity generated in the United States. All fossil fuel plants work similarly: The fuel is burned and heats water until the water turns to steam, which turns a turbine and produces electricity. A coal-fired power plant is pictured here.

2 Inside the power plant, coal is ground in a pulverizing mill to the fineness of talcum powder. This allows the coal to burn more efficiently. The ground coal is then burned in a large furnace, producing extremely high heat. The smoke from the burning of the coal tends to be "dirty"— that is, containing dirt, grit, and other pollution. Before the smoke is released into the atmosphere through smokestacks, it is sent through a precipitator, which removes some of the pollution.

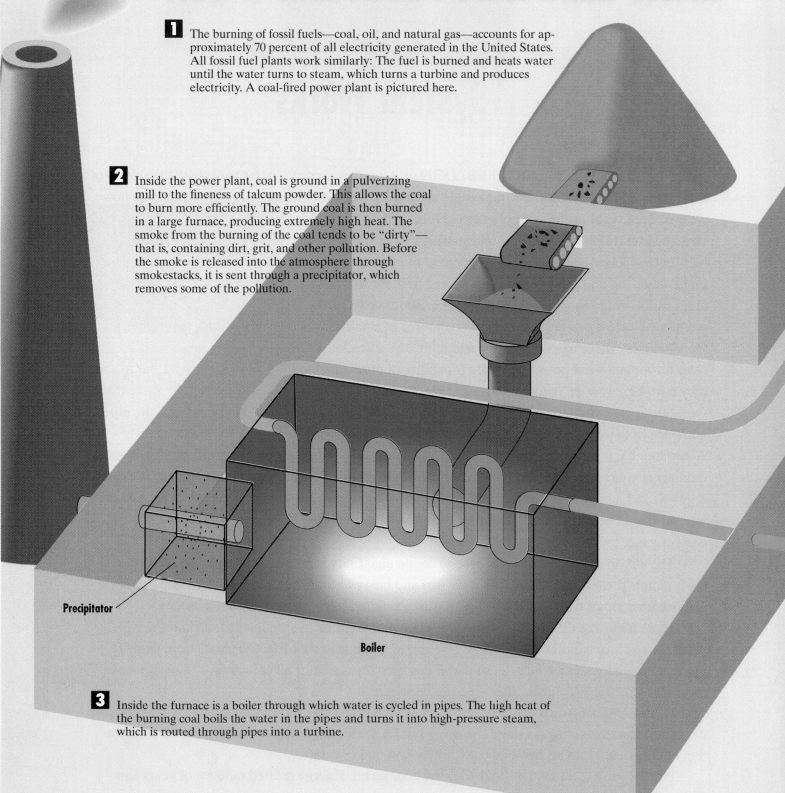

Precipitator

Boiler

3 Inside the furnace is a boiler through which water is cycled in pipes. The high heat of the burning coal boils the water in the pipes and turns it into high-pressure steam, which is routed through pipes into a turbine.

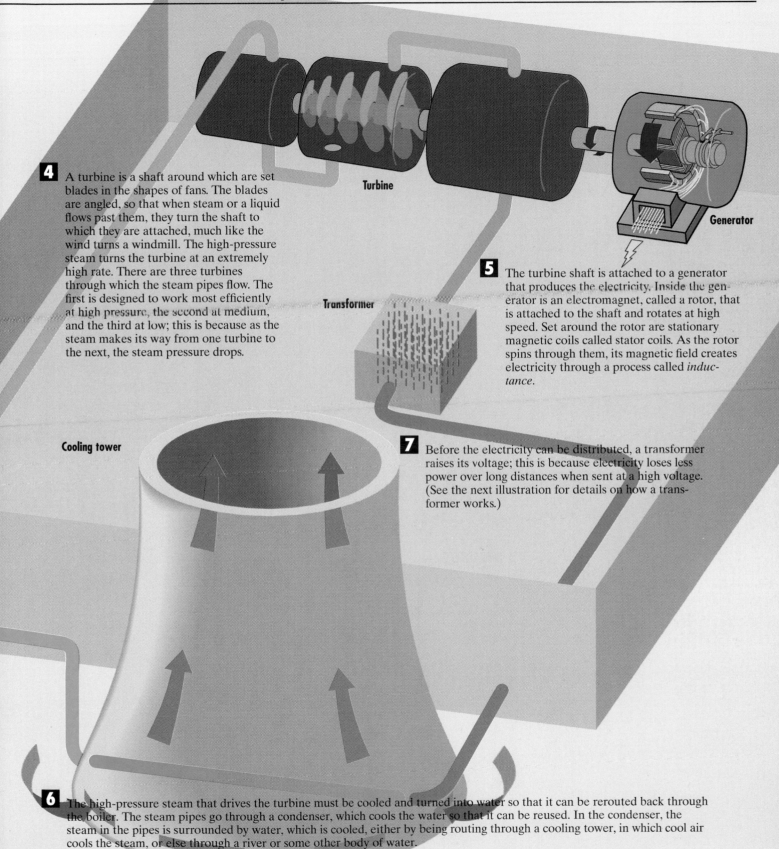

Turbine

4 A turbine is a shaft around which are set blades in the shapes of fans. The blades are angled, so that when steam or a liquid flows past them, they turn the shaft to which they are attached, much like the wind turns a windmill. The high-pressure steam turns the turbine at an extremely high rate. There are three turbines through which the steam pipes flow. The first is designed to work most efficiently at high pressure, the second at medium, and the third at low; this is because as the steam makes its way from one turbine to the next, the steam pressure drops.

Generator

5 The turbine shaft is attached to a generator that produces the electricity. Inside the generator is an electromagnet, called a rotor, that is attached to the shaft and rotates at high speed. Set around the rotor are stationary magnetic coils called stator coils. As the rotor spins through them, its magnetic field creates electricity through a process called *inductance*.

Transformer

Cooling tower

7 Before the electricity can be distributed, a transformer raises its voltage; this is because electricity loses less power over long distances when sent at a high voltage. (See the next illustration for details on how a transformer works.)

6 The high-pressure steam that drives the turbine must be cooled and turned into water so that it can be rerouted back through the boiler. The steam pipes go through a condenser, which cools the water so that it can be reused. In the condenser, the steam in the pipes is surrounded by water, which is cooled, either by being routing through a cooling tower, in which cool air cools the steam, or else through a river or some other body of water.

How the Power Delivery System Works

1 The electricity from inside a power plant is delivered to homes and businesses via a power delivery system. This system changes the voltage of the electricity at key points, depending upon whether a high or low voltage is required. High-voltage electricity is best for long-distance transmission, while low-voltage electricity is required for use in the home.

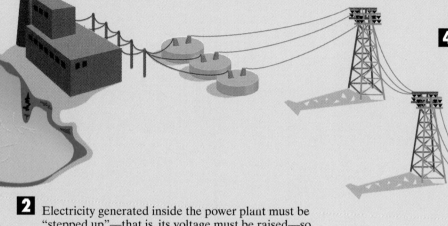

4 The high-voltage electricity is transmitted long distances over lines made of aluminum or copper, which are suspended on high transmission towers made of metal or wood. The electricity is transmitted at nearly the speed of light, 186,000 miles per second. Insulators made of porcelain and glass stop the lines from contacting each other or the tower.

2 Electricity generated inside the power plant must be "stepped up"—that is, its voltage must be raised—so that it can be transmitted most efficiently at long distances. A transformer turns the electricity into voltages of 765 million volts and above for long-distance transmission. The exact voltage level is determined by the distance the electricity will travel and the amount of electricity that will flow through the wires.

Transformer

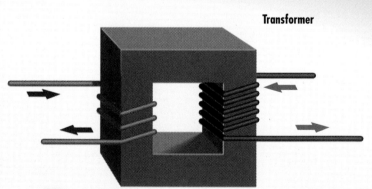

3 Transformers work on the principle of inductance: Coils are wrapped around opposing sides of a metal core, and electricity is transmitted from one set of coils (the input coils) to the other (the output coils). When there are more input coils than output coils, the electricity's voltage will be increased as it travels between the coils. When there are more output coils than input coils, the voltage will be decreased. For example, if there are twice as many output coils than input coils, the voltage will be decreased by half. Note that it is only voltage—not the total amount of electricity flowing through the coils—that is altered by the transformer.

5 The high-voltage electricity flows into a substation transformer. This transformer "steps down" (that is, reduces) the voltage of the electricity so that it can be distributed in a local area. The voltage is reduced to 23,000 volts and distributed directly to large industrial sites that require high-voltage electricity, or it is reduced to between 2,300 and 4,000 volts for local distribution. This lower-voltage electricity is now sent to distribution lines, which carry it to individual neighborhoods. The lines can be either overhead or buried underground, as they are in many cities.

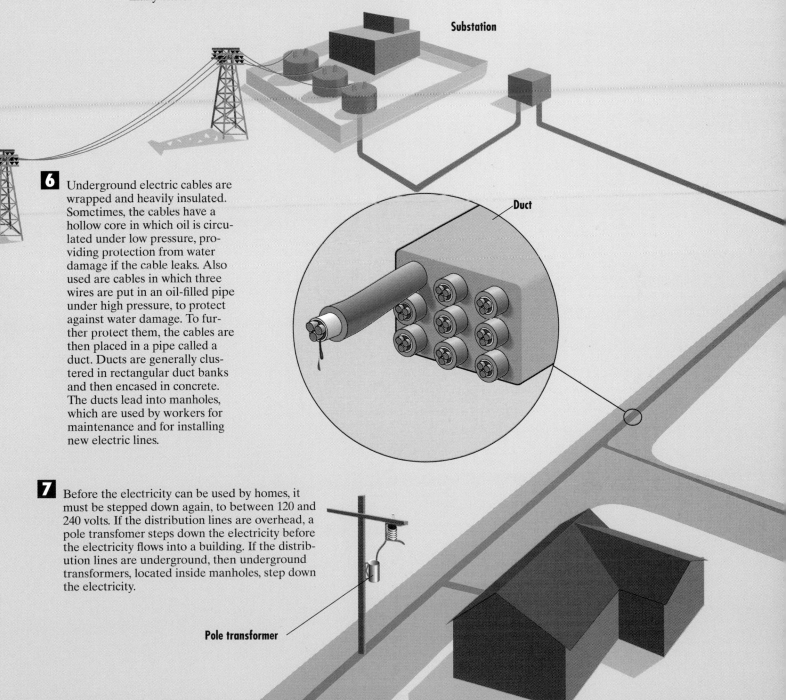

Substation

6 Underground electric cables are wrapped and heavily insulated. Sometimes, the cables have a hollow core in which oil is circulated under low pressure, providing protection from water damage if the cable leaks. Also used are cables in which three wires are put in an oil-filled pipe under high pressure, to protect against water damage. To further protect them, the cables are then placed in a pipe called a duct. Ducts are generally clustered in rectangular duct banks and then encased in concrete. The ducts lead into manholes, which are used by workers for maintenance and for installing new electric lines.

Duct

7 Before the electricity can be used by homes, it must be stepped down again, to between 120 and 240 volts. If the distribution lines are overhead, a pole transformer steps down the electricity before the electricity flows into a building. If the distribution lines are underground, then underground transformers, located inside manholes, step down the electricity.

Pole transformer

How Electricity Flows through Your Home

1 Electricity is brought into your house from an overhead utility pole or via underground as three wires twisted together or, in older houses, separate. The wires run first through an electric meter, which measures the amount of electricity you use, and then into the main service panel, generally found on a basement wall.

3 Each of your house's circuits consists of three wires that run from the main service panel to appliances and outlets. One is a *hot wire* (or live wire) that carries the electricity generated by the power company. This wire is often covered by black insulation, although it can be any color except white, gray, or green. A neutral wire, covered by white or gray insulation, completes a circuit when connected to the hot wire, and allows electricity to begin flowing. A *ground wire*, which is either bare copper or else covered with green insulation, protects against shocks. Homes built before the 1950s may not have this ground wire.

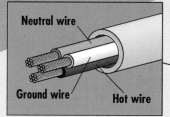

Neutral wire

Ground wire   Hot wire

2 The main service panel serves several purposes. Through separate circuits, it routes the electricity to different sections of the house. It also ensures that too much electricity doesn't flow through any individual circuit, causing the wiring to overheat, melt, or ignite. In older homes, a fuse in the fusebox of the panel is attached to each circuit, with all the electricity for the circuit flowing through that fuse. When too much electricity is flowing through, the fuse melts or burns out, and the circuit connection is cut. In newer homes, a circuit breaker serves the same purpose. When too much electricity flows, a switch is automatically flipped, and the flow to that circuit is cut off.

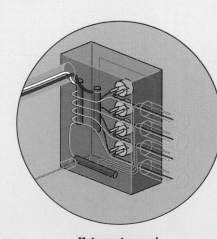

Main service panel

4 As a way to guard against shocks, modern plugs that fit into outlets are *polarized*. You can fit a two-pronged polarized plug into an outlet in only one way—one blade of the plug is wide and fits into only one slot, while the other is narrow and notched. The wide blade attaches to the neutral wire, while the narrow one attaches to the hot wire. In the case of a three-pronged plug, you can only fit the plug in one way as well, guarding against accidental shocks. In the days before polarized plugs, if you plugged a plug into an outlet, you might have attached the hot blade to the neutral wire and vice versa. This could potentially lead to shocks.

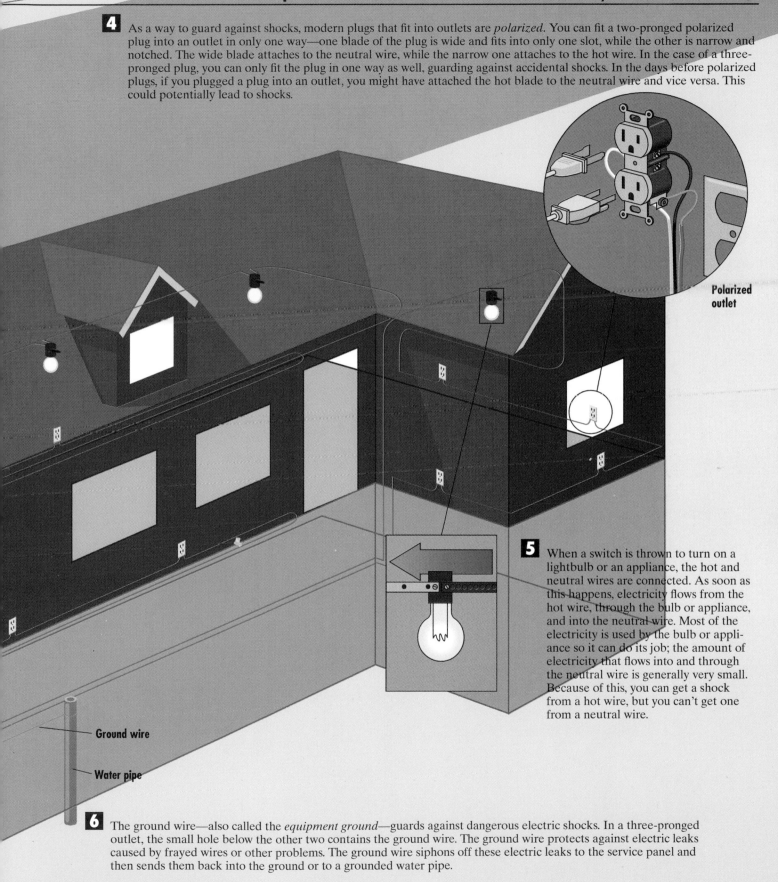

Polarized outlet

5 When a switch is thrown to turn on a lightbulb or an appliance, the hot and neutral wires are connected. As soon as this happens, electricity flows from the hot wire, through the bulb or appliance, and into the neutral wire. Most of the electricity is used by the bulb or appliance so it can do its job; the amount of electricity that flows into and through the neutral wire is generally very small. Because of this, you can get a shock from a hot wire, but you can't get one from a neutral wire.

Ground wire

Water pipe

6 The ground wire—also called the *equipment ground*—guards against dangerous electric shocks. In a three-pronged outlet, the small hole below the other two contains the ground wire. The ground wire protects against electric leaks caused by frayed wires or other problems. The ground wire siphons off these electric leaks to the service panel and then sends them back into the ground or to a grounded water pipe.

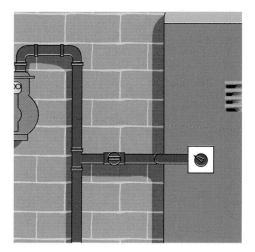

CHAPTER

4

How the Gas Delivery System Works

BEFORE ELECTRICITY, THERE was natural gas. It was used as far back as 900 B.C. in China as a heat source to evaporate sea water to make salt. Europeans began using gas much later. By around 1790, it was used to light city streets in England. In the early 1820s, a town on the shores of Lake Erie—Fredonia, New York—pioneered the use of gas to light city streets in the United States.

Today, natural gas—most commonly methane—is used primarily for heating and cooking, and it is valued as one of the cleanest sources of energy. The natural gas we use today was formed millions of years ago, when plant and animal organisms were buried at the bottom of oceans and lakes. Over millions of years this organic matter was converted by heat and pressure into natural gas, which now lies within the earth's core and is drawn to the surface through wells.

Not all gas pumped from the wells can be used directly; it often must be processed first to remove nitrogen, carbon dioxide, sulfur compounds, and water. Other gases, such as propane and butane, can also often be extracted from the gas pumped from the wells. These gases are bottled and delivered to people who have no way of getting methane gas because they don't live near natural gas pipelines.

Gas is generally transported to cities from gas fields via a system of underground transmission pipelines that can be thousands of miles long. The Northern Lights pipeline is 3,400 miles long and brings gas from the West Siberian fields in the Arctic Circle to the cities of eastern Europe. In the United States, most of our gas comes from gas fields in Texas, Louisiana, and Alaska, although we also get gas from other places, notably Canada. While much of our gas is transported via pipelines, gas is also shipped, especially from Alaska and the Middle East, in huge tankers that hold liquefied natural gas. Gas is liquefied by being cooled to –256° Fahrenheit, and then is stored in these tankers. A single tanker can carry up to 2.5 billion cubic feet of gas.

In the United States, there are nearly 2 million miles of gas lines, and many of these lines were built during World War II. Transporting natural gas via pipeline over long distances requires sizable metal pipes, which average about 4 feet in diameter, although some pipes can measure over 6½ feet. In order to be transmitted over long distances, gas must be placed under very high pressure—generally 1,000 pounds per square inch. In order to maintain that high pressure, machinery

How Gas Is Distributed in the City

1 Natural gas comes from wells drilled into the ground and is brought to cities for distribution in one of two ways: shipped in huge tankers in liquid form, or sent from one of 200,000 wells to cities by a vast system of underground welded steel pipes. These gas transmission lines stretch underground from gas fields in Texas and Canada to as far away as California, and from Louisiana to as far away as New England. The cost of building these tranmission lines is almost a million dollars per mile. Compression stations along the way use engines to create high pressure—generally 1,000 pounds per square inch—to force the gas through the lines to their final destination.

2 Once the gas reaches the city, it is often stored in liquid form (liquified natural gas, or LNG) in large, aboveground tanks. Storing gas as a liquid saves an enormous amount of storage space: 615 cubic feet of natural gas in its gaseous state is the equivalent of one cubic foot of liquid gas.

3 To distribute the gas to households and businesses in the city, the LNG is warmed and thus returned to its normal gaseous state. It travels via underground pipes to buildings in the city. These gas distribution lines were initially built out of metal, although newer pipes are made out of plastic, which is cheaper, lasts longer, and is easier to install. Main pipes bring the gas down city streets, while smaller service pipes deliver the gas to individual buildings.

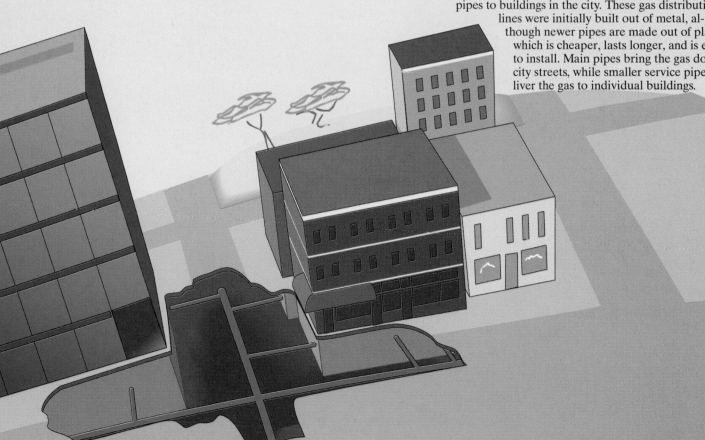

4 In order for the gas distribution network to work properly, certain pressures have to be maintained within the pipes to deliver the gas to buildings. The pressure is regulated by special underground checkpoints, which are located in pairs in manholes approximately 25 feet apart. The gas main in each manhole runs through a regulator, which increases or decreases the flow of the gas automatically, depending upon the pressure that the gas in the pipe is under. Filters remove debris and particles from the gas that could clog up the regulator. At times, the regulator needs to vent gas; it does so through a vertical exhaust pipe that runs to the street.

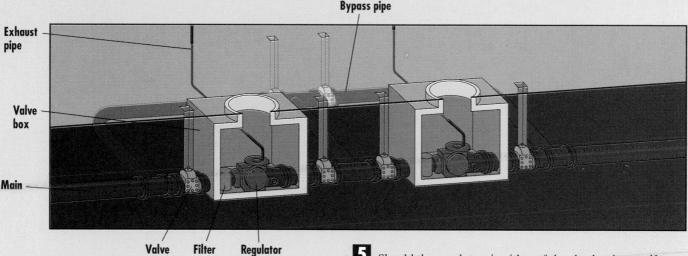

Exhaust pipe

Bypass pipe

Valve box

Main

Valve   **Filter**   **Regulator**

5 Should the regulators in either of the checkpoints malfunction, gas can be routed around one or both of them by turning on or off valves located in main and bypass pipes. The valves either cut gas off, or allow it to flow through the main and bypass pipes, depending upon whether a regulator works or needs to be bypassed. To turn on and off the valves, gate keys are lowered into valve boxes and turned. In addition to being found near checkpoints, these valve boxes are also located on service pipes that feed the buildings in the city.

Service pipe

6 Service pipes bring gas directly into the basements of buildings. Gas meters measure how many cubic feet of gas a building uses. Inside, a main gas valve can be turned off to halt the flow of gas into the building, should repairs be needed. Valves leading to individual gas appliances such as stoves, furnaces, and water heaters also allow each of these appliances to be shut off separately, so that gas can still flow through the rest of the building.

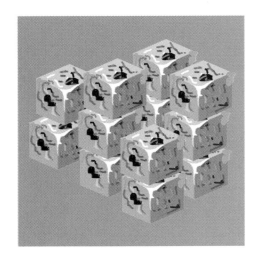

Cleaning the City: Sewers and Garbage Collection

OF ALL PARTS of the city hidden from us, the least talked about are those that get rid of our wastes, whether they be garbage, human waste, or the grime that washes off city streets in rainstorms. But without this hidden infrastructure, cities and towns would be far different from what they are today—far less pleasant and far more dangerous.

While disposal systems may seem mundane, their development has played a large part not only in making cities livable, but also in fighting disease and increasing our life expectancy. For it is modern sanitation, possibly as much as modern health technology, that has freed us from the plagues of the past.

The two most important disposal systems are those that carry away sewage and garbage. Sewers carry human wastes from buildings into huge pipes. In the past, sewage would then be discharged untreated into rivers, streams, and the ocean. In more recent times, laws require that sewage first be cleaned in treatment plants. This requirement has led to the cleanup of rivers and waterways across the United States—although the job still isn't finished. One major problem is that in many cities the storm drain system—the series of underground pipes that carries away water from rainstorms and melting snow and ice—feeds directly into the sewage system. In times of heavy rain, so much water floods the combined sewage/storm drain system that the treatment plant can't keep up with it, and so sewage and street runoff are dumped into waterways without being treated. To combat this, many cities are separating the systems.

Increasingly, the major pollutant of waterways is no longer sewage but water that runs off city streets. Solvents, heavy metals, and lawn chemicals are just some of the dangerous materials that flow through storm drains into nearby rivers and, ultimately, the ocean. In fact, urban runoff is now the primary source of water pollution in Los Angeles County and endangers Chesapeake Bay and San Francisco Bay, to name only a few of many examples. Federal regulations have been enacted to solve the problem, and lawsuits are underway where necessary to force cities to comply.

Garbage—specifically, what to do with it—is just as large a problem because space for landfills is vanishing. However, there is a solution that is increasingly being put to use: recycling. Many cities and towns now mandate that newspapers, cans, bottles, and plastics be recycled, and many other municipalities have begun voluntary recycling programs. Recycling cuts down on the need for new landfills and also reduces our consumption of energy and natural resources—benefitting the environment as a whole. By recycling we are not only saving open space, we are also saving the air we breathe and the forests we walk in.

The Storm Drain and Sewer Systems

Two types of systems can be found beneath city streets. The sewer system carries wastewater away from homes and buildings, while the storm drain system drains water from storms or melting ice and snow. Both systems depend on gravity—the pipes slope downward, allowing gravity to force the water to flow. The two systems sometimes are connected, which can lead to pollution problems, as explained below.

Lateral

Submain

Main

1 Individual pipes from homes and buildings carry wastewater from homes into laterals. These laterals flow into a larger pipe called a submain. Submains flow into a still-larger pipe called a main. Mains in turn flow into an interceptor, which is the huge pipe that leads into a sewage treatment plant, where the wastewater and sewage are treated.

2 Manholes are located wherever sewer pipes change direction or grade. They are also located where several submains flow into a main, in which case the manhole does not contain pipes but exposed passageways designed to avoid blockages. Manholes are large enough that workers can climb into them to clean them.

3 When sewer pipes get blocked or develop leaks, there are many ways to clean them. In one of the newest ways, a video camera is mounted on a small, remote-controlled wheeled cart. Workers can see from the camera where the problem occurs. If the leak or blockage is small enough, they can operate remote-controlled tools mounted on the same cart as the camera to repair the crack in the pipes.

4 Catch basins in streets carry water into the storm drain system during storms. Storm drain pipes must be much larger than sewer pipes because they need to carry tremendous amounts of water in a short amount of time.

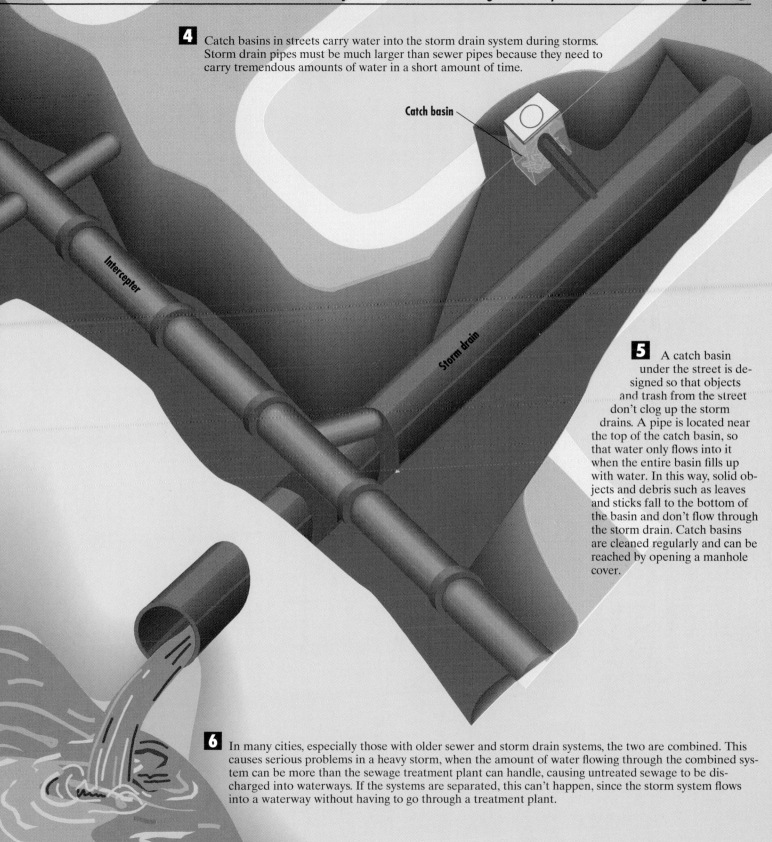

Catch basin

Intercepter

Storm drain

5 A catch basin under the street is designed so that objects and trash from the street don't clog up the storm drains. A pipe is located near the top of the catch basin, so that water only flows into it when the entire basin fills up with water. In this way, solid objects and debris such as leaves and sticks fall to the bottom of the basin and don't flow through the storm drain. Catch basins are cleaned regularly and can be reached by opening a manhole cover.

6 In many cities, especially those with older sewer and storm drain systems, the two are combined. This causes serious problems in a heavy storm, when the amount of water flowing through the combined system can be more than the sewage treatment plant can handle, causing untreated sewage to be discharged into waterways. If the systems are separated, this can't happen, since the storm system flows into a waterway without having to go through a treatment plant.

How a Sewage Treatment Plant Works

Large pipes bring raw sewage to a sewage treatment plant. The most modern plants put the sewage through three stages of treatment: primary, in which large objects, nonbiodegradable objects, and 60 percent of the solids, 30 percent of organic matter, and up to 15 percent of nutrients are removed from sewage; secondary, in which 90 percent of the remaining organic matter and 30 percent to 50 percent of the nutrients are removed; and tertiary, in which chemicals like phosphorus and any remaining dissolved solids are removed.

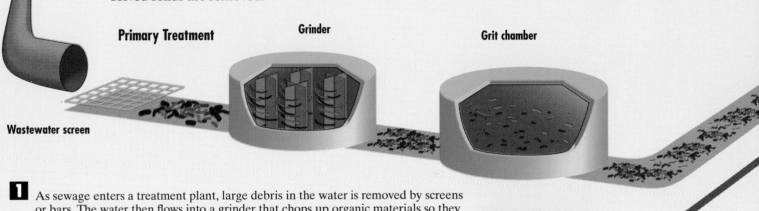

Primary Treatment　　**Grinder**　　**Grit chamber**

Wastewater screen

1 As sewage enters a treatment plant, large debris in the water is removed by screens or bars. The water then flows into a grinder that chops up organic materials so they can be more easily treated. The water then passes through a grit chamber where sand, silt, gravel, and similar matter is removed.

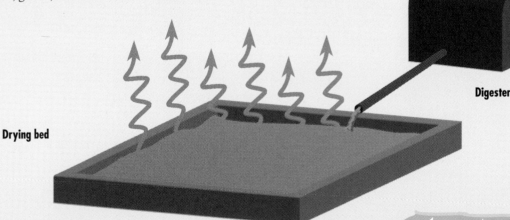

Digester

Drying bed

3 The sludge is put into a digester. Enzymes and then acid-producing bacteria are added to the sludge in the digester. These bacteria turn the sludge into organic acids. Other types of bacteria then convert these organic acids into methane and carbon dioxide. The remaining digested sludge is poured onto sand drying beds where water percolates through the sand and evaporates into the air, leaving behind dried sludge that can be used as fertilizer or a soil conditioner. Some treatment plants sell the fertilizer.

2 Much of the organic matter in the water is removed through the next step—*sedimentation*. The water flows into a sedimentation tank, where organic materials settle to the bottom and are then disposed of. Sedimentation can be aided when chemicals such as aluminum sulfate are added to wastewater. This causes solids that are suspended in the water to attach to one another and fall to the bottom of the sedimentation tank. The solid materials that settle in a sedimentation tank are called *sludge*.

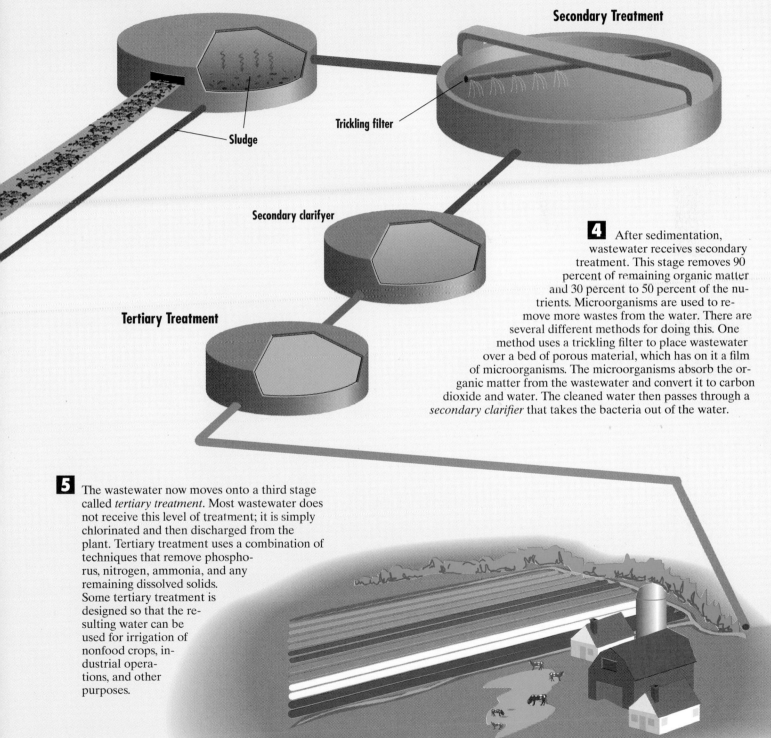

Sedimentation tank

Sludge

Trickling filter

Secondary Treatment

Secondary clarifyer

Tertiary Treatment

4 After sedimentation, wastewater receives secondary treatment. This stage removes 90 percent of remaining organic matter and 30 percent to 50 percent of the nutrients. Microorganisms are used to remove more wastes from the water. There are several different methods for doing this. One method uses a trickling filter to place wastewater over a bed of porous material, which has on it a film of microorganisms. The microorganisms absorb the organic matter from the wastewater and convert it to carbon dioxide and water. The cleaned water then passes through a *secondary clarifier* that takes the bacteria out of the water.

5 The wastewater now moves onto a third stage called *tertiary treatment*. Most wastewater does not receive this level of treatment; it is simply chlorinated and then discharged from the plant. Tertiary treatment uses a combination of techniques that remove phosphorus, nitrogen, ammonia, and any remaining dissolved solids. Some tertiary treatment is designed so that the resulting water can be used for irrigation of nonfood crops, industrial operations, and other purposes.

Recycling and Garbage Collection

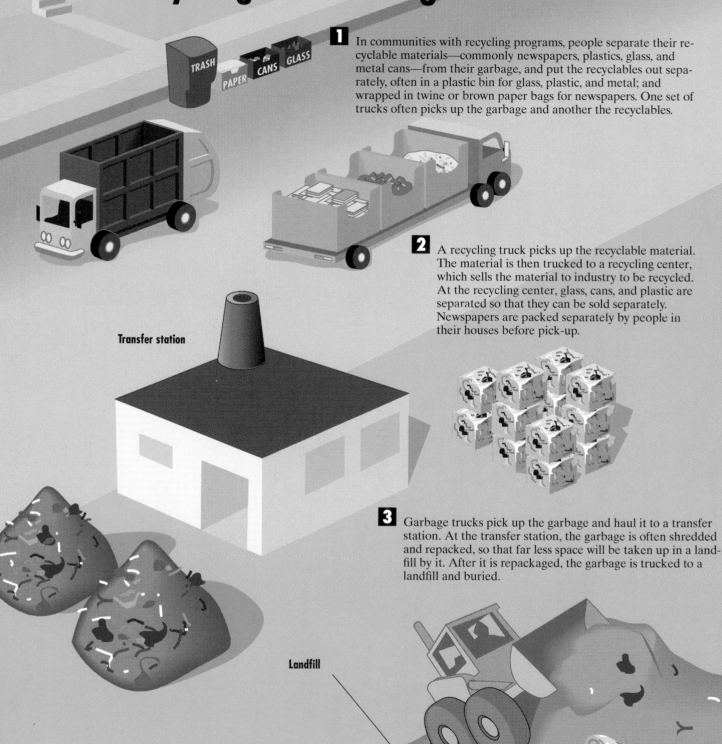

1 In communities with recycling programs, people separate their recyclable materials—commonly newspapers, plastics, glass, and metal cans—from their garbage, and put the recyclables out separately, often in a plastic bin for glass, plastic, and metal; and wrapped in twine or brown paper bags for newspapers. One set of trucks often picks up the garbage and another the recyclables.

2 A recycling truck picks up the recyclable material. The material is then trucked to a recycling center, which sells the material to industry to be recycled. At the recycling center, glass, cans, and plastic are separated so that they can be sold separately. Newspapers are packed separately by people in their houses before pick-up.

3 Garbage trucks pick up the garbage and haul it to a transfer station. At the transfer station, the garbage is often shredded and repacked, so that far less space will be taken up in a landfill by it. After it is repackaged, the garbage is trucked to a landfill and buried.

TRASH

PAPER CANS GLASS

Transfer station

Landfill

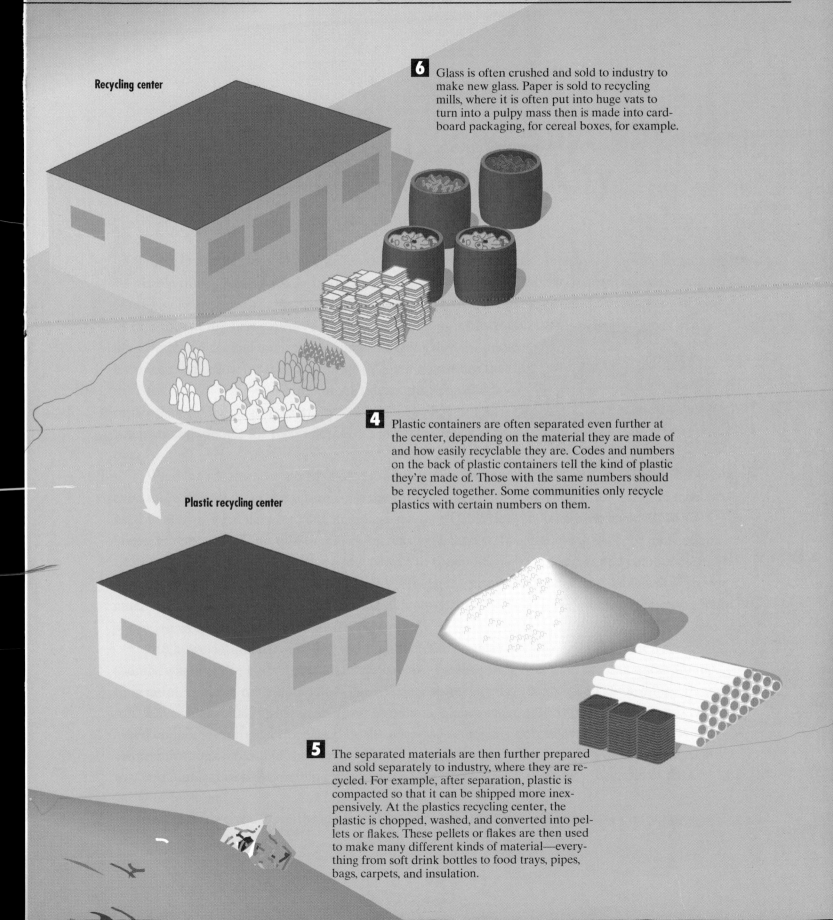

Recycling center

6 Glass is often crushed and sold to industry to make new glass. Paper is sold to recycling mills, where it is often put into huge vats to turn into a pulpy mass then is made into cardboard packaging, for cereal boxes, for example.

Plastic recycling center

4 Plastic containers are often separated even further at the center, depending on the material they are made of and how easily recyclable they are. Codes and numbers on the back of plastic containers tell the kind of plastic they're made of. Those with the same numbers should be recycled together. Some communities only recycle plastics with certain numbers on them.

5 The separated materials are then further prepared and sold separately to industry, where they are recycled. For example, after separation, plastic is compacted so that it can be shipped more inexpensively. At the plastics recycling center, the plastic is chopped, washed, and converted into pellets or flakes. These pellets or flakes are then used to make many different kinds of material—everything from soft drink bottles to food trays, pipes, bags, carpets, and insulation.

How Cable TV Works

1 A cable TV system has a head end that receives all the television channels it will distribute to its subscribers. The head end receives these signals from satellites as well as from regular transmissions from local TV stations. Typically, the system receives signals from a number of satellites, each of which sends numerous channels, often several dozen or more. The sytem receives transmissions from local television stations on tall antennas.

Satellite dish

Satellite dish

Antenna

Modulator

Amplifier

2 The TV signals need to be transformed so that they are suitable for transmission to subscribers over TV cables. Each signal goes through its own modulator and amplifier. The amplifier pumps up the signal so that it's strong enough to be received by subscribers. The modulator codes each individual signal so that it a cable receiver can tune in to it.

Outer jacket

Braided copper shielding

Plastic Insulation

Copper conductor

Coaxial cable

Trunk station

3 The signals are all sent simultaneously through coaxial cable. Coaxial cable allows for the simultaneous transmission of many signals because it can be kept free of outside electrical interference. It's made free of this interference because a jacket of woven copper braid shields the copper center conductor from outside interference. The conductor is also insulated with plastic.

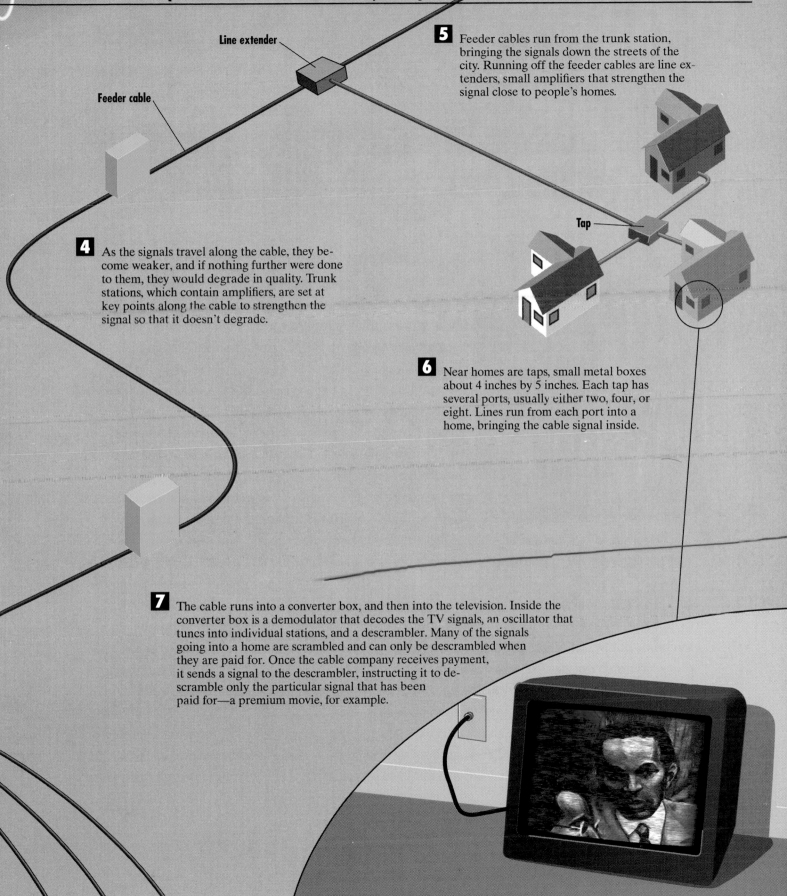

Line extender

Feeder cable

5 Feeder cables run from the trunk station, bringing the signals down the streets of the city. Running off the feeder cables are line extenders, small amplifiers that strengthen the signal close to people's homes.

Tap

4 As the signals travel along the cable, they become weaker, and if nothing further were done to them, they would degrade in quality. Trunk stations, which contain amplifiers, are set at key points along the cable to strengthen the signal so that it doesn't degrade.

6 Near homes are taps, small metal boxes about 4 inches by 5 inches. Each tap has several ports, usually either two, four, or eight. Lines run from each port into a home, bringing the cable signal inside.

7 The cable runs into a converter box, and then into the television. Inside the converter box is a demodulator that decodes the TV signals, an oscillator that tunes into individual stations, and a descrambler. Many of the signals going into a home are scrambled and can only be descrambled when they are paid for. Once the cable company receives payment, it sends a signal to the descrambler, instructing it to descramble only the particular signal that has been paid for—a premium movie, for example.

A Cutaway View of an Apartment Building

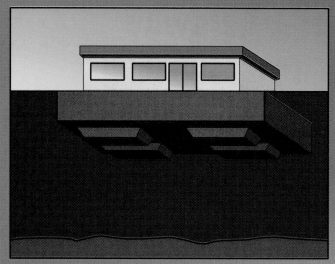

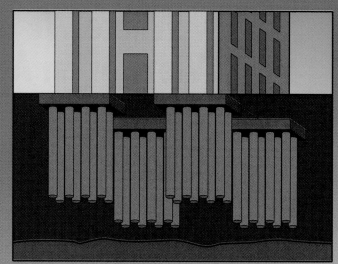

1 Beneath apartment buildings—and any other large buildings in the city—are foundations that take the weight of the building above them and redistribute it to the material below so that the least possible stress is put on the building. There are several types of foundations. In a floating foundation, pictured here and often used in smaller buildings and houses, the entire building is supported by a concrete slab.

2 In a friction pile foundation, as shown here, piles of concrete, reinforced concrete, and steel-encased concrete are driven into the ground in clusters. (In earlier days even wood was used.) The clusters of piles are connected to concrete caps, which hold up the building. Friction piles are used when the foundation is not going to rest on bedrock; instead, the piles distribute the weight of the building to the ground.

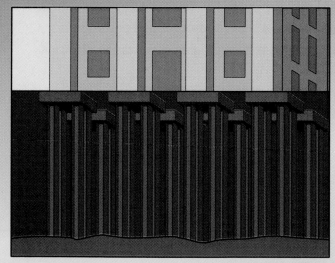

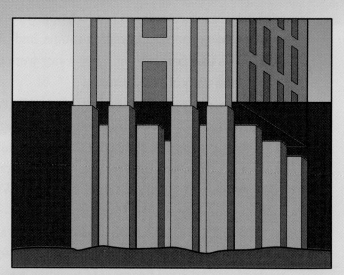

3 Bearing piles are sunk into bedrock, clay, and sometimes firm soil, into which they distribute the weight of the building. Since bedrock is sometimes located deep beneath a city, bearing piles may have to be sunk two hundred feet or more. The most common types of bearing piles are steel pipes filled with concrete and steel beams in the shape of an *H*. They are clustered and attach to concrete slabs that support the building.

4 Piers are similar to bearing piles in that they distribute the weight of the building they support into bedrock, clay, or firm soil. They are typically large shafts of concrete. They are not clustered as are piles, and so do not need a concrete cap. Instead, they hold up the building directly.

5 The pillars and beams of smaller apartment buildings may be made of reinforced concrete, since that material is relatively flexible and strong and does not contract or twist easily. To make reinforced concrete, concrete is poured around iron rods and allowed to dry. Between pillars and beams, other materials, such as brick or prefabricated walls, are usually used instead of reinforced concrete.

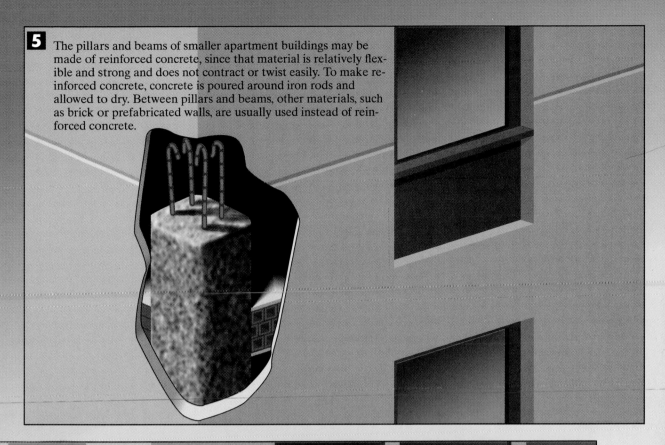

6 In an apartment building of more than 30 or so stories, using heavy reinforced concrete for pillars and beams may cause problems because the foundation may be unable to support the weight of the building. Instead, builders use much lighter metal beams. Typically these are *I*-shaped, allowing other building material like cement or brick to be inserted for easier construction.

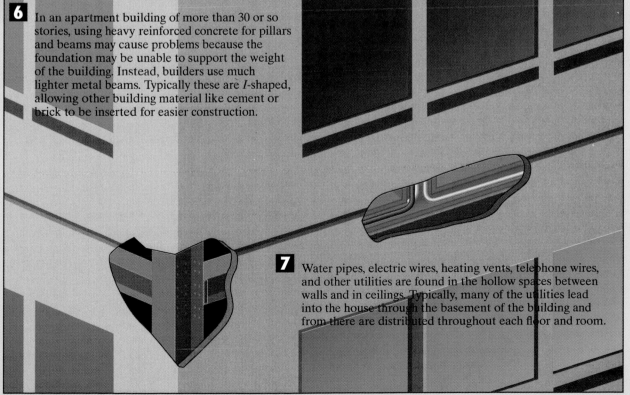

7 Water pipes, electric wires, heating vents, telephone wires, and other utilities are found in the hollow spaces between walls and in ceilings. Typically, many of the utilities lead into the house through the basement of the building and from there are distributed throughout each floor and room.

The City as an Ecosystem

1 The city is not different from the rest of nature: It is an ecosystem like any other, and the same laws of nature apply to it. Many things make the city's ecosystem unique, though, all stemming from one fact: Cities have been built for the convenience of a single species, *homo sapiens*.

3 In general, cities receive more precipitation than the nearby nonurban areas around them. The warm air that rises in a city because of the heat island effect has the ability to hold more moisture because it contains more dust, particles, and smog. This wet, rising warm air creates fog and precipitation.

2 Cities are warmer and less sunny than the surrounding countryside. They're warmer because buildings, streets, and sidewalks absorb heat from the sun and radiate it back into the air—turning the city into a *heat island*. Cities are less sunny because dust, smog, and other pollutants cut down on the amount of sunlight reaching city streets.

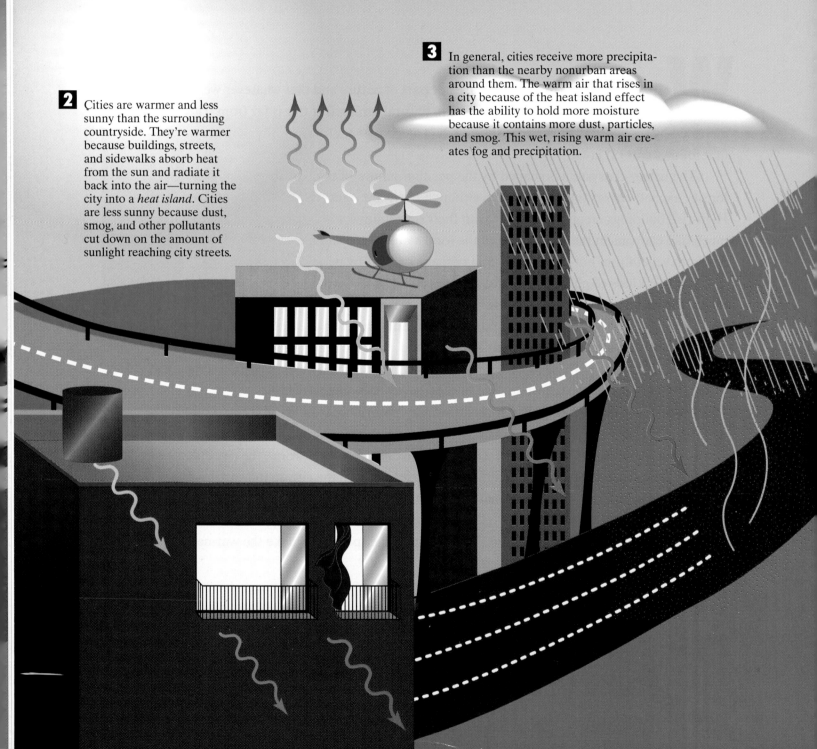

4 The presence of garbage and litter has created ecological niches for many kinds of city animals. Bees in the city, for example, often get their food not from flowers, as in the wild, but from discarded soda cans and half-eaten fruit. Rats feed on garbage and refuse, and birds like pigeons eat castoff food and are also fed by people.

5 Many birds and animals that thrive in the city today initially came from the countryside. As early as the fourteenth century, people in London began noticing that pigeons—descendants of doves that lived in the wild—were beginning to move into the city. Interestingly, many city animals in the United States today initially came from other countries. The starling is an example.

6 The number of animals living in the city is surprisingly high. In fact, there are those who believe that the total number of animals in a city exceeds the number that live in an area of comparable size in the wild. The difference, however, is that very few species of animals live in the city, so wildlife is less varied than in the countryside.

7 The suburbs provide a very different ecosystem. Here there is more greenery and vegetation and more varied ecological niches than in the city. Because of this, there is more varied wildlife here as well, although not as varied as in the wild. As in the city, the animals that thrive here are those that are "opportunistic"—they can live in a variety of places and eat a wide variety of foods. A notable example of this kind of opportunistic species is the raccoon.

How Wildlife Lives in the City

North American cities provide a refuge for an unlikely animal: the peregrine falcon, an endangered species. The falcons were released by biologists, who hoped that the cities would prove amenable to the birds and help preserve them from extinction. The falcons live on top of skyscrapers, which resemble their natural habitat of rocky cliffs. They ride the city's air currents in search of their prey—city-dwelling birds like the pigeon and the starling.

Many of the most common birds seen in U.S. cities are not native to North America. The house sparrow, for example, was imported into New York City in 1852 to fight an infestation of a caterpillar called the cankerworm, which was stripping the city's trees bare. The starling was brought into America in 1890 by a man who wanted the United States to be home to every bird mentioned in Shakespeare. Pigeons arrived even earlier, with the colonists. Originally they lived on farms; then they moved into the cities, where they are now ubiquitous.

The unique environment of the city attracts some birds that once lived only in the wild. During warm-weather days, heat builds up in the city because buildings absorb and then release heat. The hot air rises, carrying with it the insects living in the city and its parks, to be eaten by birds like the nighthawk and the chimney swift, once prairie-dwellers but now nesting on roofs and in chimneys.

The red-tailed hawk, another predator, also makes its home in some cities. Some of these birds have been seen in the Boston Common and Public Garden, where they eat squirrels and rodents. In the spring, with the return of warm weather, they migrate north. Red-tailed hawks also live in other cities, including Los Angeles.

Not all wildlife in the city is welcomed: One of the most common animals is one that few people want to see—the rat. Rats feed on garbage left in cans without lids; they live in subways and feed on scraps and litter; they live and feed in sewers.

The Urban Forest: How Trees Make the City More Livable

Trees are invaluable resources for the city, doing everything from cleaning the air to providing shade and saving energy for city homes and businesses. They have financial benefits as well: A recent study found that if Chicago planted 95,000 trees, the city and its residents would save a net total of $38 million in heating, cooling, and environmental clean-up costs. There are an estimated 60 million street trees in U.S. cities, and one estimate holds that the cities can accommodate 60 million more.

Trees play a major role in cleaning urban air pollution. Leaf tissues absorb toxic chemicals and elements of smog and air pollution, including ozone, sulfur dioxide, carbon monoxide, and heavy chemicals. Smoke particles and particulates, as well as dust, ash, and pollen, collect on leaves and are washed away by rain and snow. Trees also help fight global warming by absorbing carbon dioxide—one the main causes of the greenhouse effect—and releasing oxygen; one estimate holds that a single healthy city tree absorbs 13 tons of carbon dioxide a year.

Heat-absorbing buildings, concrete, and asphalt all serve to turn cities into "heat islands" in the summer, raising their temperatures as much as 15 degrees above the surrounding countryside. Trees help cool the city by reflecting from 10 to 25 percent of radiation away and by transpiring water, which cools the nearby area. A single tree can transpire up to 100 gallons of water a day, providing the cooling equivalent of running five air conditioners 20 hours a day in the summer.

Trees also reduce air conditioning costs by shading buildings in the summer. By protecting buildings and houses against winter winds, they also keep buildings warmer in the winter, and so reduce fuel bills. Estimates for savings range from 10 to 50 percent in air-conditioning costs and from 15 to 25 percent in heating costs. Trees placed facing west windows have been found to be most efficient for reducing energy costs.

Trees reduce urban noise pollution. Sounds are absorbed and deflected by the canopy of leaves, tree branches, and tree trunks, making for a more livable city. In addition to cutting down on harsh noises, trees add to the urban environment pleasing sounds of their own—wind whistling through their branches songs of birds.

The aesthetic appeal of trees provides an unquantifiable lift to cities. Birds and animals can be seen in them, bringing a bit of the countryside to the city. Fall colors, spring flowers, and other aspects of the natural world make the city a more appealing place to live.

Dangers Facing the Urban Forest—and How to Save It

City trees can die if their root systems are cut, trimmed, or disrupted. This can happen when trenches are dug near them to lay down pipes or cables for public utilities. The trees generally don't die immediately, but instead die a slow death, which may take several years. In Great Britain, many recent tree deaths have been attributed to the massive amount of underground cable being laid for cable television systems. To solve the problem, care needs to be taken not to disturb root systems when digging trenches or repainring streets.

The urban forest is dangerously homogenous—very few species of trees live in cities. In most cities, two to five species types of trees make up over two-thirds of the entire population. For example, in Brooklyn, New York, two kinds of trees—the Norway maple and the London plane—compose over 65 percent of all trees in the city. This homogeneity is dangerous because a single disease can wipe out a large percentage all at once, as has already happened in recent times. The graceful American elm was planted in huge numbers in cities, and urban forests were decimated when Dutch elm disease destroyed them. In order to guard against this, no single tree species should compose more than 5 percent of the population of city trees, specialists say.

City trees on the whole don't live as long as their counterparts in the wild because of the city's harsh environment. Air pollution harms trees, as does the summer's severe heat. Volunteer organizations have sprung up in American cities to care for trees and to stop vandalism.

Nature's cycle of turning dead leaves and branches into nutrients and protection for trees is circumvented in cities. In forests, dead vegetative matter decomposes into nutrient-rich humus that contains elements like carbon, nitrogen, and phosphorus that feed trees. In the city, on the other hand, dead branches and leaves are removed, so trees are often slowly starved of vital nutrients. To solve the problem, many cities collect leaves and branches from trees, allow them to decompose, and then use the compost to feed city trees. Milwaukee, for example, has been composting since 1936. Dead branches and leaves are also chipped into pieces and used as layers of mulch to protect city trees.

The Ecology of a House

JUST AS THE CITY is a living environment, so are the homes we live in. Natural laws do not suddenly end at our doorsteps; they apply inside a home's walls as well as outside of them.

A variety of ecological niches exist inside our homes. There's a hidden world of life there, and much of what's alive is unwelcome. House mice nest there and feed off food scraps. Cockroaches, originally tropical insects, thrive because of the warmth and the ready availability of food to scavenge. Insects such as silverfish eat common household items such as glue, paste, and newspapers.

You may think of your house as a refuge against the pollution that can be found outside. Unfortunately, that's not true; air pollution may be greater inside your house than outside of it. Synthetic carpets, insulation, and furniture made from plywood and particle board release formaldehyde fumes. Household pesticides can be dangerous. Common household products such as oven cleaners, furniture polish, and caulking include many potentially dangerous chemicals. And levels of pollutants caused by combustion—such as sulfur oxides, nitrogen oxides, and hydrocarbons—may be very high in homes due to improperly working furnaces or wood stoves. These pollutants can do more than make you uncomfortable: Many people are killed every year by carbon monoxide poisoning.

Many people have houseplants in their homes. These plants do more than look pretty. They can clean up the environment in your home. Plants absorb carbon dioxide and release oxygen, and they also absorb pollutants such as formaldehyde, making for a cleaner indoor environment.

The lawn outside your home is also an environment unto itself. Many birds live there because of the easy availability of food from gardens, bird feeders, and garbage cans. Attics, ledges, and chimneys provide nesting places for squirrels, raccoons, and birds. And the presence of garbage cans means that opportunistic species that can eat a wide variety of foods—such as the raccoon—thrive here. Increasingly, animals commonly thought of only as wild are sighted in suburbia. Deer have become more common, bear sightings are not infrequent, and even mountain lions and coyotes have been known to drop in. That's because suburbs are sprouting up in places that until recently have been wild.

The Ecology of a House

Homes provide an ideal environment for many kinds of insects. The ubiquitous cockroach was originally a tropical insect. Homes, because of their warmth and because of the availability of crumbs and garbage that roaches can scavenge, provide an ideal environment for them. Silverfish thrive in homes because they can eat glue, paste, wallpaper, paper, magazines, sugar, and cereals, as well as other household items.

House mice are also unwelcome visitors that have come in from the wild and found a unique environmental niche in the home. They build nests out of common household materials such as paper, cloth, and packing material, and they eat crumbs, garbage, and leftovers.

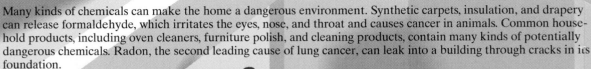

Many kinds of chemicals can make the home a dangerous environment. Synthetic carpets, insulation, and drapery can release formaldehyde, which irritates the eyes, nose, and throat and causes cancer in animals. Common household products, including oven cleaners, furniture polish, and cleaning products, contain many kinds of potentially dangerous chemicals. Radon, the second leading cause of lung cancer, can leak into a building through cracks in its foundation.

Household plants contribute to a healthy indoor environment. They absorb dangerous gases such as formaldehyde, benzene, trichloroethylene (TCE) and other VOCs (volatile organic chemicals). For example, chrysanthemums have been found to remove formaldehyde fumes, and English ivy removes benzene. Plants also absorb carbon dioxide and release oxygen.

Backyards provide homes for a variety of animals. Animals such as raccoons, birds, and squirrels live on ledges and in chimneys . Omnivorous mammals, such as the raccoon, eat many different kinds of foods and therefore thrive in backyards, where they can eat refuse from garbage cans. Even animals thought of as wild, such as bears, at times forage in the suburbs because of the availability of food in garbage cans.

CHAPTER

Smog: The Curse of the Cities

SMOG, ONE OF THE curses of our cities, sits as a thick haze over many places in the summer. Smog is created when a variety of pollutants from automobiles and industry mix, sit in the air overhead, and in the presence of heat and sunlight undergo chemical reactions that create ozone, among other chemicals. The result is called photochemical smog. When high above the earth, ozone shields us from harmful ultraviolet radiation. But when it's found close to the ground, it's toxic and can harm the cardiopulmonary system, causing pulmonary congestion, chest pain, and general impairment of the function of the lungs.

Ozone is certainly not the only chemical in smog that has harmful effects. Nitrogen oxides lower resistance to respiratory infections and irritate the lungs. Sulfur dioxide is particularly hazardous—and even deadly—for people with cardiovascular and respiratory diseases. Volatile organic compounds can cause nausea and irritate the lungs and eyes. Particulates—small particles of dust, soot, and other material—may cause cancer and can also exacerbate cardiovascular diseases.

The primary culprit behind smog is the automobile. The chemicals, pollutants, gases, particulates, and smoke the auto emits go a long way toward creating the yellowish, brownish, foul-smelling air with which so many of us are too familiar. Industry adds to the problem with its own mix of lethal chemicals and gases that escape its smokestacks.

There is some good news, however. Federal laws designed to decrease air pollution have dramatically cut smog throughout the country. Laws requiring cleaner-burning automobiles and cleaner industry have improved the air. There's no doubt that cities are freer of air pollution today than at any time in recent memory.

That doesn't mean that they're clean enough, though. During the peak smog months in the summer, many cities still simmer in a poisonous soup of pollutants.

If we look only to the government, though, the problem will never be solved. If we each personally reduce our use of the automobile—if we use public transportation, or bicycles, or walk—we'll go a long way toward reducing air pollution. And then our cities will become even more livable than they are today.

How Smog Is Created

Nitrogen oxides (NO_x) react with oxygen (O_2) in the air and produce nitrogen dioxide (NO_2). Sunlight and the corresponding warmth are conducive to converting nitrogen oxides into nitrogen dioxides. Nitrogen dioxide irritates the lungs, and can cause or exacerbate respiratory diseases such as bronchitis and pneumonia. It can also make people more vulnerable to diseases such as influenza.

SO_2

O_2

NO_x

NO_2

NO_x

The kind of smog that is generally found in cities today is called photochemical smog. It is formed when various pollutants mix, react in the presence of sunlight, and then form new toxic chemicals. Smog is the resulting mix of original pollutants plus new chemicals. The process begins when factories burn fossil fuels, especially coal, and release sulfur dioxide (SO_2) and particulates, (soot and other small particles). Sulfur dioxide damages the respiratory system, and is a component of acid rain. Particulates irritate the respiratory system, and may also carry toxic materials such as heavy metals deep into the lungs.

SO_2

NO_x

SO_2

NO_x

NO_x

CO

NO_x

CO

NO_x

CO

NO_x

NO_x

CO

CO

NO_x

Automobiles emit many different types of air pollutants that contribute to smog, notably nitrogen oxides (NO_x) and carbon monoxide (CO). Before the elimination of lead in gasolines in the United States, much lead was released as well. Carbon monoxide causes drowsiness, lethargy, and headaches, and can also lead to angina attacks. Lead affects the nervous system and lowers children's learning ability.

Smog becomes most dangerous when temperature inversions occur. In a temperature inversion, a warm layer of air moves in over a cooler layer of smog. Since warm air rises, this new layer sits on top of the existing smog, trapping it so that it cannot leave. This allows smog to build up over days to dangerous levels. Los Angeles is prone to these inversions because nearby mountains allow warm air to flow in and trap smog in lower layers.

$$O_2 + O$$

$$O_3 \quad NO_2$$

$$VOC$$

Nitrogen dioxide absorbs energy in the form of sunlight. In the presence of volatile organic compounds, NO_2 induces the formation of ozone (O_3). Because more ozone is formed in the presence of heat and sunlight, the highest concentrations of ozone are present generally during the hot, bright days of summer. When high in the atmosphere, ozone protects us from some of the sun's harmful ultraviolet radiation. But when close to the earth as it is in smog, ozone breaks down human tissue and attacks the respiratory system. It reduces lung function and causes coughing, shortness of breath, chest pain, and congestion; it is especially dangerous to people with existing cardiorespiratory problems.

VOC   VOC

Volatile organic compounds (VOCs) are released from many sources, such as chemical manufacturing, dry cleaning, paints and solvents, evaporation from automobile fuel tanks, and automobile exhaust. VOCs cause headaches, nausea, and eye, nose, and throat irritations at low doses. At high concentrations, such as those that someone might be exposed to in an industrial setting, they can cause liver and kidney damage.

24 HR Drycleaning and Laundry

Wood's Barbeque
Take out   *Delivery*

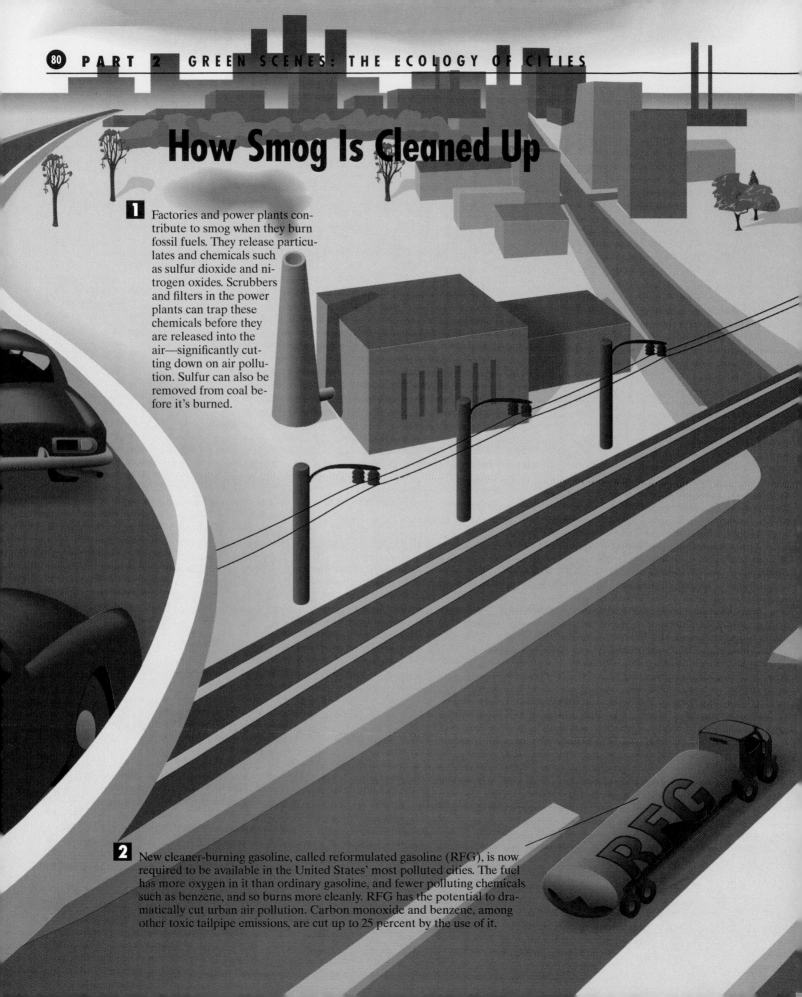

How Smog Is Cleaned Up

1 Factories and power plants contribute to smog when they burn fossil fuels. They release particulates and chemicals such as sulfur dioxide and nitrogen oxides. Scrubbers and filters in the power plants can trap these chemicals before they are released into the air—significantly cutting down on air pollution. Sulfur can also be removed from coal before it's burned.

2 New cleaner-burning gasoline, called reformulated gasoline (RFG), is now required to be available in the United States' most polluted cities. The fuel has more oxygen in it than ordinary gasoline, and fewer polluting chemicals such as benzene, and so burns more cleanly. RFG has the potential to dramatically cut urban air pollution. Carbon monoxide and benzene, among other toxic tailpipe emissions, are cut up to 25 percent by the use of it.

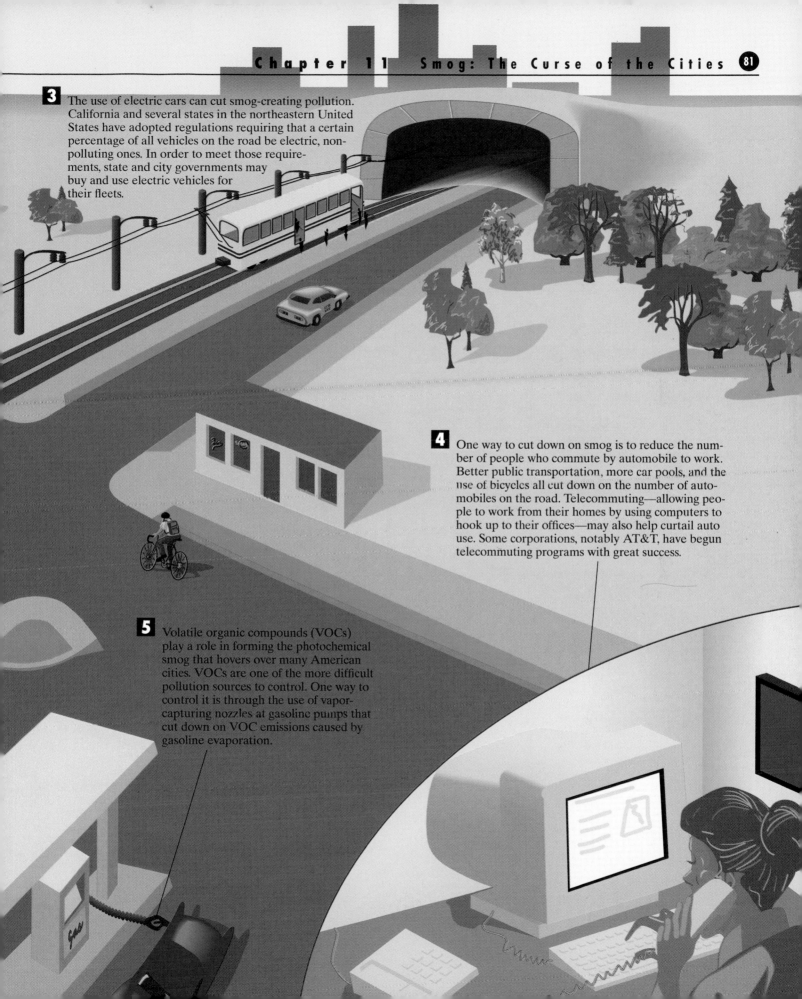

3 The use of electric cars can cut smog-creating pollution. California and several states in the northeastern United States have adopted regulations requiring that a certain percentage of all vehicles on the road be electric, nonpolluting ones. In order to meet those requirements, state and city governments may buy and use electric vehicles for their fleets.

4 One way to cut down on smog is to reduce the number of people who commute by automobile to work. Better public transportation, more car pools, and the use of bicycles all cut down on the number of automobiles on the road. Telecommuting—allowing people to work from their homes by using computers to hook up to their offices—may also help curtail auto use. Some corporations, notably AT&T, have begun telecommuting programs with great success.

5 Volatile organic compounds (VOCs) play a role in forming the photochemical smog that hovers over many American cities. VOCs are one of the more difficult pollution sources to control. One way to control it is through the use of vapor-capturing nozzles at gasoline pumps that cut down on VOC emissions caused by gasoline evaporation.

The Ecology of Factories and Office Buildings

BY NOW, IT'S a given that factories and power plants affect the environment in very dramatic ways. Acid rain, global warming, toxic waste, the landfill crisis…the list could go on. The price of industrial might has often been environmental degradation.

Many cities are dotted with symbols of this degradation: smokestacks rising high into the sky, belching air-polluting fumes. And the cities themselves suffer the consequences in the form of heavily polluted air. In the last two decades, though, this unfortunate scenario has begun to change. Environmental regulations have forced factories and electric plants to dramatically curb the pollution coming out of their smokestacks. Because of that, today's factories are far cleaner and more efficient than in the past.

It's not only in the United States that factories are becoming cleaner and more efficient—in fact, America isn't even the world leader in the field. The United States' two main industrial competitors—Japan and Germany—are far more advanced. And while critics of environmental regulation may have you believe that a cleaner environment means a weaker economy, those two industrial powerhouses prove the exact opposite. They have found that building cleaner factories means building more efficient factories as well, which in turn means greater profits. By burning less fuel—and so polluting less—factories cut their operating costs, often dramatically. By using recycled material, they pollute less and also reduce the cost of raw materials. And by turning waste products into products that can be sold and used—such as by cleaning the pollutant sulfur dioxide from waste gas and turning it into gypsum—they gain a new revenue stream.

Our buildings don't only affect the outdoor environment—they also create indoor environments of their own in which millions of people work each day. These environments are not always clean—in fact, in many cases the indoor environment is dirtier and more dangerous than the one outside. One example of this is sick building syndrome, in which the indoor environment causes disease and discomfort.

Industry and commerce no longer need be an enemy of the environment. In today's city—and increasingly in tomorrow's city—a cleaner environment can also mean a healthier economy.

An Environmentally Correct Factory

Many factories are finding that reducing pollution and conserving energy help not only the environment, but the bottom line as well. A perfect example can be found in the thriving Japanese steel industry, which has invested $21 billion since 1980 in environmental protection and energy-saving technology.

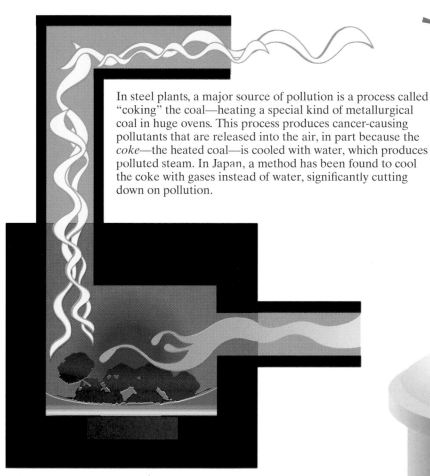

In steel plants, a major source of pollution is a process called "coking" the coal—heating a special kind of metallurgical coal in huge ovens. This process produces cancer-causing pollutants that are released into the air, in part because the *coke*—the heated coal—is cooled with water, which produces polluted steam. In Japan, a method has been found to cool the coke with gases instead of water, significantly cutting down on pollution.

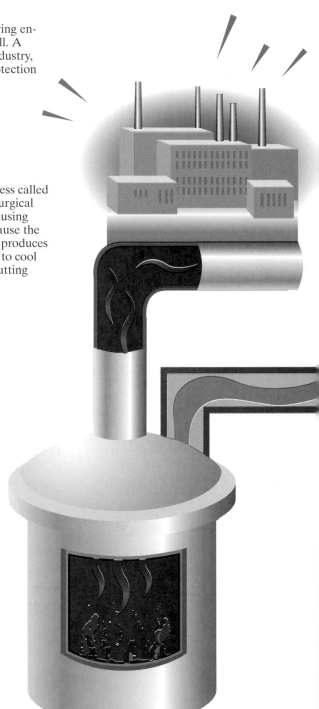

In many factories, the heat produced in a boiler is released into the air as waste instead of being used. One estimate holds that only about one-third of the heat generated in factories is actually used; the rest is wasted. Some factories, notably those in Germany, have begun reusing this "waste" heat, by heating homes or the factory itself, or by generating electricity from it.

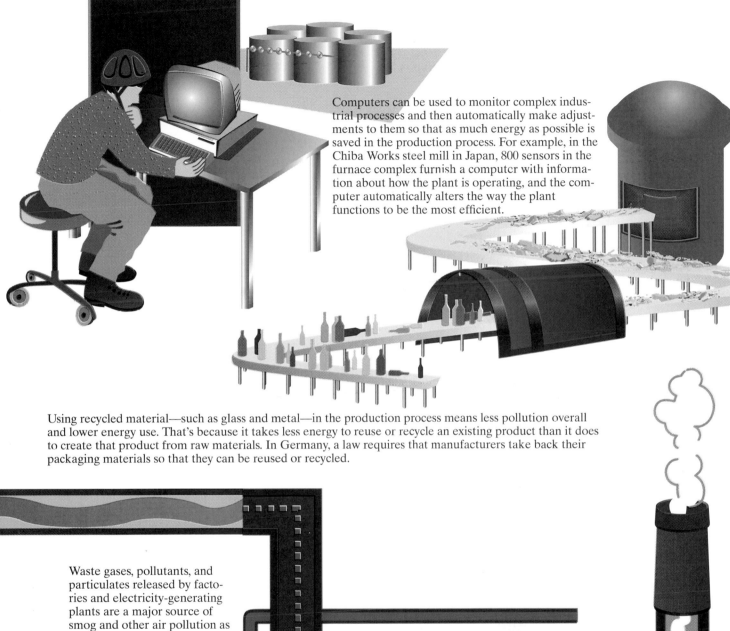

Computers can be used to monitor complex industrial processes and then automatically make adjustments to them so that as much energy as possible is saved in the production process. For example, in the Chiba Works steel mill in Japan, 800 sensors in the furnace complex furnish a computer with information about how the plant is operating, and the computer automatically alters the way the plant functions to be the most efficient.

Using recycled material—such as glass and metal—in the production process means less pollution overall and lower energy use. That's because it takes less energy to reuse or recycle an existing product than it does to create that product from raw materials. In Germany, a law requires that manufacturers take back their packaging materials so that they can be reused or recycled.

Waste gases, pollutants, and particulates released by factories and electricity-generating plants are a major source of smog and other air pollution as well as of acid rain. These pollutants can be cleaned by special scrubbers or other anti–air pollution equipment. For details on how these work, see the next page.

How Air Pollution Clean-Up Systems Work

A variety of ways have been found to remove particulates and pollutants, such as sulfur dioxide, from the gases and smoke released into the atmosphere through smokestacks in factories and power plants. These waste gases are known as flue gases. Sulfur dioxide in particular is a problem because it is a primary cause of acid rain. Two of the most common ways to remove pollution and particulates—wet scrubbers and electrostatic precipitators—are pictured here.

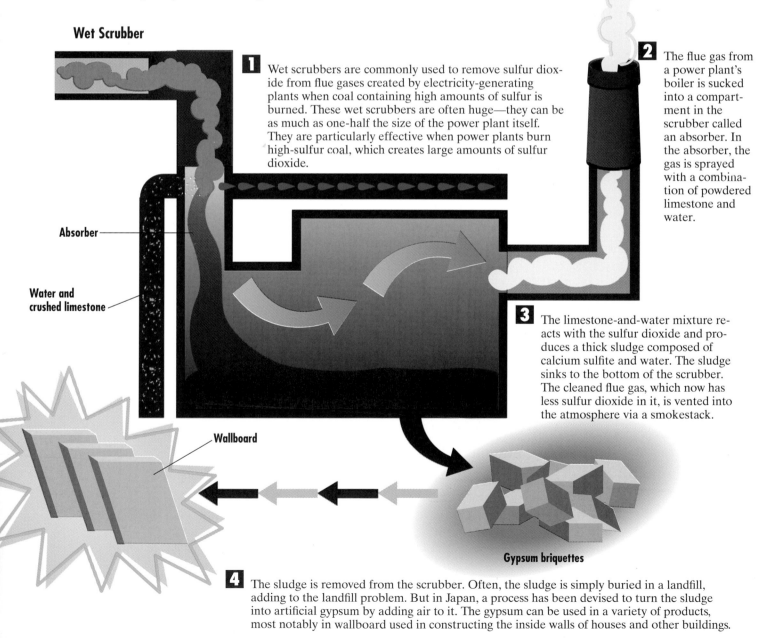

Wet Scrubber

1 Wet scrubbers are commonly used to remove sulfur dioxide from flue gases created by electricity-generating plants when coal containing high amounts of sulfur is burned. These wet scrubbers are often huge—they can be as much as one-half the size of the power plant itself. They are particularly effective when power plants burn high-sulfur coal, which creates large amounts of sulfur dioxide.

2 The flue gas from a power plant's boiler is sucked into a compartment in the scrubber called an absorber. In the absorber, the gas is sprayed with a combination of powdered limestone and water.

Absorber

Water and crushed limestone

3 The limestone-and-water mixture reacts with the sulfur dioxide and produces a thick sludge composed of calcium sulfite and water. The sludge sinks to the bottom of the scrubber. The cleaned flue gas, which now has less sulfur dioxide in it, is vented into the atmosphere via a smokestack.

Wallboard

Gypsum briquettes

4 The sludge is removed from the scrubber. Often, the sludge is simply buried in a landfill, adding to the landfill problem. But in Japan, a process has been devised to turn the sludge into artificial gypsum by adding air to it. The gypsum can be used in a variety of products, most notably in wallboard used in constructing the inside walls of houses and other buildings.

5 Electrostatic precipitators work on a completely different principle than do scrubbers—they use electric charges to remove particulates from flue gases. When flue gas flows into an electrostatic precipitator it receives a negative electric charge, which induces a negative charge in the particulates. Some advanced precipitators use microprocessors to sense the composition of the flue gases and then automatically change the amount of electric charge for maximum efficiency.

Electrostatic Precipitator

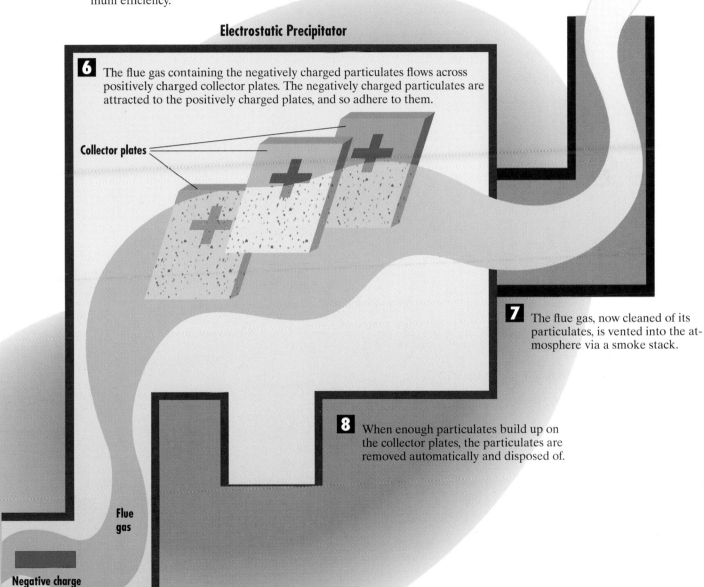

6 The flue gas containing the negatively charged particulates flows across positively charged collector plates. The negatively charged particulates are attracted to the positively charged plates, and so adhere to them.

Collector plates

7 The flue gas, now cleaned of its particulates, is vented into the atmosphere via a smoke stack.

8 When enough particulates build up on the collector plates, the particulates are removed automatically and disposed of.

Flue gas

Negative charge

What Causes Sick Building Syndrome

Sick building syndrome is a catchall name for what happens when pollutants and irritants inside a building cause any of a variety of health problems in its occupants, such as irritation of the eyes, nose, and throat; nausea; allergic reactions; and flulike symptoms. The Environmental Protection Agency (EPA) estimates that 30 percent of all buildings and homes in the United States contain enough pollutants to affect people's health.

Many buildings erected or rehabilitated since the 1970s are extremely airtight—so much so that many of them do not even have windows that can be opened. These buildings were designed to save energy, so that heat and air-conditioned air would not escape from them. But this means that indoor pollutants have no chance of dissipating into the outside air, so instead they build up inside. It also means that humidity and moisture tend to stay trapped in the building, leading to the growth of mold and mildew, which commonly cause allergic reactions.

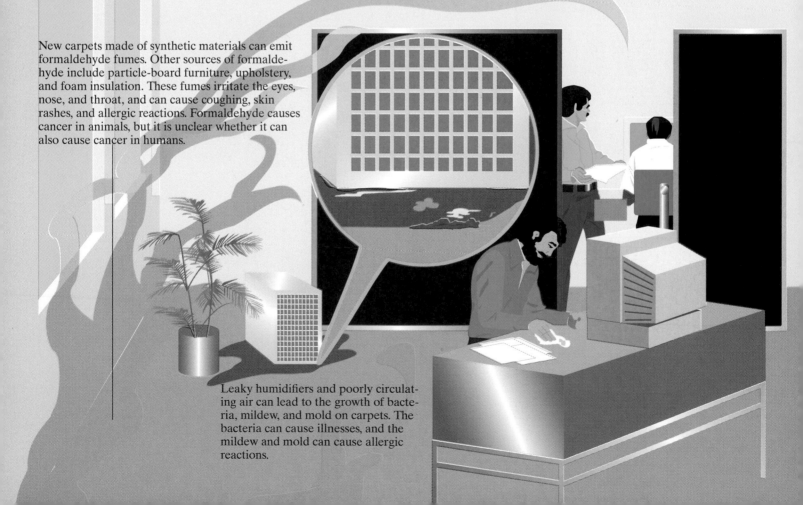

New carpets made of synthetic materials can emit formaldehyde fumes. Other sources of formaldehyde include particle-board furniture, upholstery, and foam insulation. These fumes irritate the eyes, nose, and throat, and can cause coughing, skin rashes, and allergic reactions. Formaldehyde causes cancer in animals, but it is unclear whether it can also cause cancer in humans.

Leaky humidifiers and poorly circulating air can lead to the growth of bacteria, mildew, and mold on carpets. The bacteria can cause illnesses, and the mildew and mold can cause allergic reactions.

Aspergillus niger, the microorganism that turns bathroom tiles black, can infect air-conditioning ducts and cause sick building syndrome. This microorganism reproduces by producing tiny spores. These spores are breathed into the lungs. When someone is frequently exposed to these spores, a sensitivity develops, and the person's body produces compounds called histamines whenever the spore is encountered. These histamines cause upper respiratory congestion, runny nose, and a hayfever-like reaction.

Tobacco smoke is a major indoor pollutant, and especially in buildings where the smoke does not dissipate, it can add to the problems caused by sick building syndrome. Tobacco smoke contains over 4,700 compounds, including formaldehyde, ammonia, toluene, sulfur dioxide, and phenol, as well as many toxins, carcinogens, and mutagens—material that can cause genetic damage. In addition to causing respiratory problems, this secondhand smoke also increases the risk of lung cancer, it may be a risk factor for heart disease, and it increases the chance that children will get pneumonia and bronchitis.

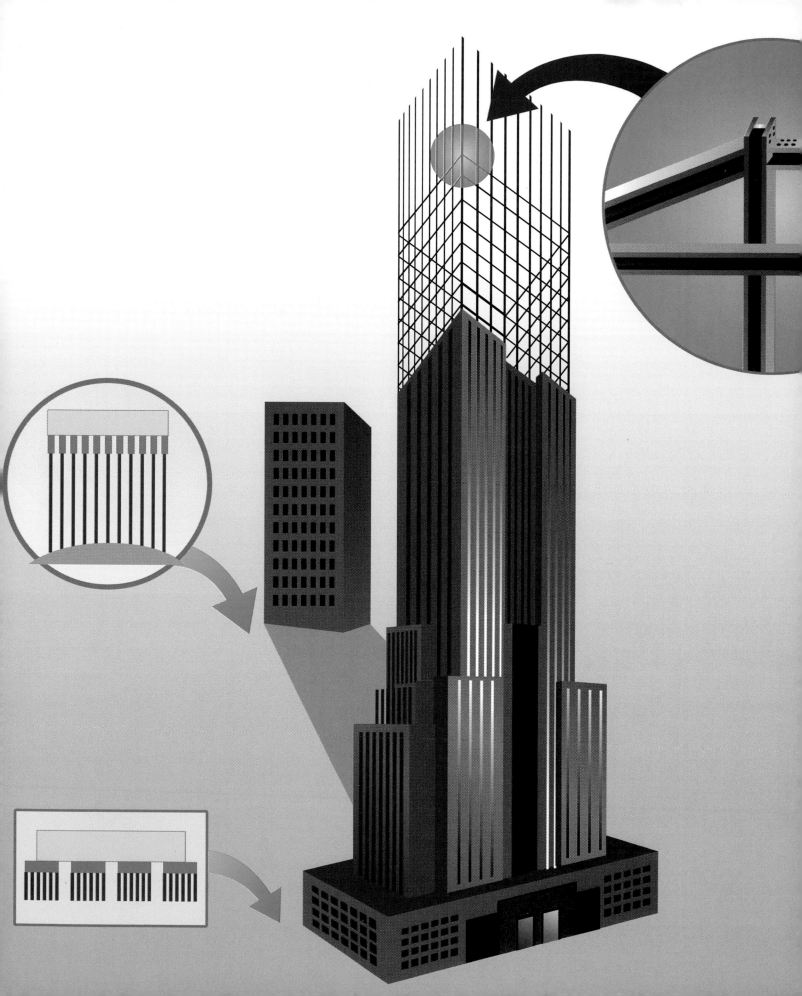

Going Up: Construction in the City

CONTENTS

CITIES NEVER STAY the same; if they remain static they die. They grow over time, and this process of growth is what gives cities much of their vitality. The city would be a very different place without the sound of jackhammers, the presence of massive pieces of earth-moving equipment, the skeletal structures slowly fleshing out before our eyes. We have an enduring fascination with the ways in which the city around us is constructed.

In fact, at first glance, the most distinguishing feature of the modern city is its sheer physical presence. Stately skyscrapers reach for the sky, bridges span waterways, tunnels burrow beneath harbors. The city's physical environment is a growing, vital thing, changing over time not just in response to the needs of people who live there, but to changes in building technology as well.

The way cities look today is due in large part to building technology made possible by the industrial revolution. For example, it was a technological development of the late nineteenth century that allowed for the construction of skyscrapers and massive suspension bridges—the ability to forge iron and steel beams. Before these beams were used, buildings were constructed of heavy materials such as stone. This allowed builders to create sturdy buildings, but there was a serious problem if one tried to build them over a certain height: They were so heavy that if built too high, they would collapse under their own weight; foundations couldn't support them. By the late nineteenth century, relatively lightweight iron and steel beams replaced traditional materials such as stone in the construction of buildings. This led to an unprecedented race toward the sky in American cities, most notably in Chicago and New York, with builders rapidly one-upping each other to erect the world's tallest building. In quick succession 20-, 60-, and 70-story skyscrapers were built, culminating with the most elegant and sweeping building of the engineer's art in 1931: the Empire State Building, which was then the tallest building in the world.

Similarly, technology altered the way that bridges were built. They too were originally made of heavy materials such as stone, so they couldn't be too large lest they collapse under their own weight. The relatively light weight and formidable strength of cast iron changed that, and in 1781 an iron bridge made of cast iron rails was built in England's industrial heartland, Coalbrookdale.

Advances in metal casting allowed for the creation of large suspension bridges. In these bridges, thick, metal cables are used, and from them are suspended lighter cables that hold up the bridge below. New York City's George Washington Bridge and San

Francisco's Golden Gate Bridge are the two best known, and among the most beautiful, of this type of bridge.

In this part of the book, we'll take a closer look at how skyscrapers, bridges, and tunnels are built.

In Chapter 13, we'll take a close look at how the modern skyscraper is constructed. We'll see that what's beneath the street is often as important as what's above it in the construction of skyscrapers, and we will look at the different kinds of foundations that make them possible. We'll see how a light inner frame of girders provides the skeleton upon which the building is constructed. And we'll see how, as the lower levels are being completed, the upper levels have not even begun to be built yet.

Chapter 14 examines how tunnels are built. There are many different techniques for doing this, but we'll look at two of the most common and most important. We'll look at how tunnels are bored underground and often underwater, through rock, silt, and other material. The tunnel recently built beneath the English Channel (connecting France and England) was built in this way, and used massive, highly automated tunnel boring machines (TBMs) to eat through rock and soil. We'll also look at sunken tube tunnels, such as one being built in Boston beneath the Boston Harbor. This amazing technology requires that huge sections of tunnel be built in factories and then sunk into trenches dug for them, where they are connected to form a long tunnel.

Finally, in Chapter 15, we'll take a close look at how suspension bridges—among the world's most elegant and awe-inspiring of structures—are built.

We'll see in this part how human ingenuity and raw necessity interact and lead to innovative building technologies that shape the modern world.

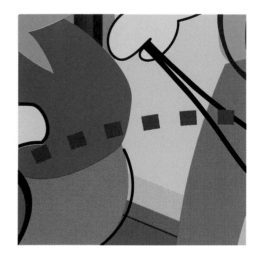

CHAPTER 13

Skyscrapers

THE MODERN AMERICAN CITY is defined largely by a single image: the distinctive silhouette of its skyscrapers outlined against the sky. The soaring towers of Manhattan are what people conjure up when they think of cities. Indeed, for many people, a modern city without a massive core of skyscrapers lit up at night is not a city at all, only a collection of suburbs lumped together willy-nilly.

The first skyscrapers were built in Chicago and New York in the late nineteenth century. New technology brought them into being. Before this time, buildings couldn't be built over a certain height because the weight of the building material, often reinforced concrete, was so great that the foundation wouldn't be able to hold up a tall building—it would collapse under its own weight. By the late nineteenth century, though, relatively light iron and steel beams replaced reinforced concrete in building frames, allowing the construction of much taller buildings.

Technology wasn't the only force driving the construction of skyscrapers—economics played a role as well. After the Great Chicago Fire leveled much of Chicago in 1871, there was a building boom, and the price of land skyrocketed. A very large building raised on a relatively small piece of land would reap greater profits than would a small building built on the same area. These economic and technological forces made Chicago home to the first skyscrapers, such as the Home Insurance Building, erected in 1885, and the 21-story Masonic Building, which was the tallest skyscraper in the world when it was constructed in 1892.

Soon after, New York City became the world's center for skyscrapers. Its 36-story Park Row building, constructed just after the turn of the century, became the world's tallest skyscraper. New York builders outdid one another in reaching for the skies: the Woolworth Building at 60 stories; the elegant art deco–influenced Chrysler Building at 77 stories; and then finally the culmination of the builder's art, the stately Empire State Building, finished in 1931, the world's tallest building for over 40 years (until the twin towers of New York's World Trade Center overtook it).

Classic skyscrapers such as the Chrysler Building and Empire State Building have a unique "stepped-back" look to them—they are broader at the base than at the top and proceed upwards in a series of steps. This is not because their designers thought the look was elegant: A 1916 New

York City building code (since changed) required that at the point where a building was 125 feet tall, it had to be less wide than the base on which it was set. Then, at the thirtieth floor, it had to be reduced in size yet again so that it was one quarter or less the size of the base of the building.

These soaring towers in many ways represent the spirit of the modern city. In medieval times, the church was civilization's driving force, so great cathedrals were constructed. Today, commerce rules, so skyscrapers—shrines to business—define the landscape of modern urban life.

How Skyscrapers Are Built

1 The foundations of skyscrapers must be strong and stable in order to support the immense weight of the buildings above them. In a *friction pile foundation*, piles of concrete, reinforced concrete, or steel-encased concrete are sunk in the ground in clusters and connected to concrete caps, which support the building. Friction pile foundations distribute the weight of the building to the ground when there is no bedrock for support. In a *bearing pile foundation,* piles made of concrete and steel are sunk into bedrock attached to concrete slabs to support the building above. Since bedrock is sometimes located deep beneath a city, bearing piles may have to be sunk 200 or more feet.

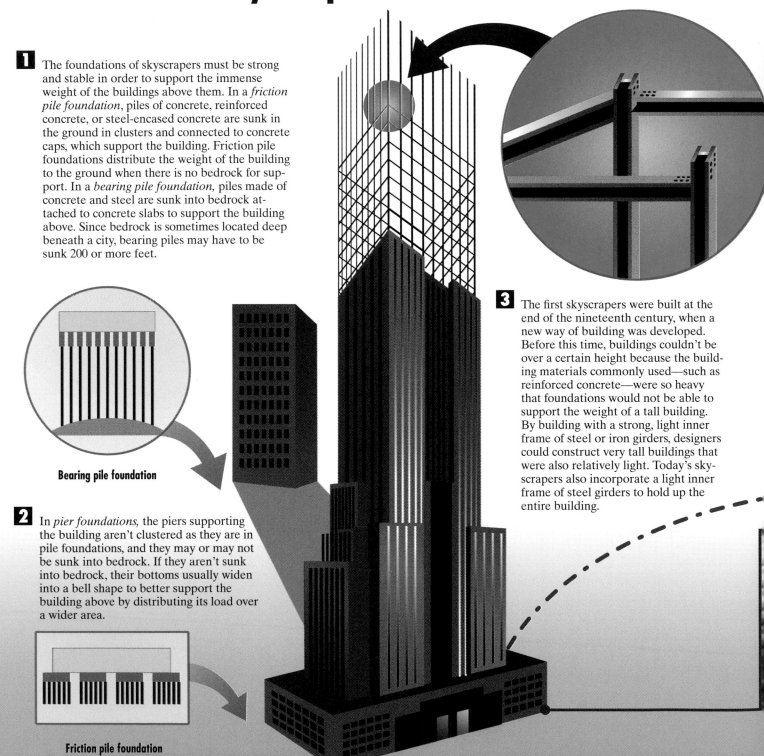

Bearing pile foundation

Friction pile foundation

2 In *pier foundations,* the piers supporting the building aren't clustered as they are in pile foundations, and they may or may not be sunk into bedrock. If they aren't sunk into bedrock, their bottoms usually widen into a bell shape to better support the building above by distributing its load over a wider area.

3 The first skyscrapers were built at the end of the nineteenth century, when a new way of building was developed. Before this time, buildings couldn't be over a certain height because the building materials commonly used—such as reinforced concrete—were so heavy that foundations would not be able to support the weight of a tall building. By building with a strong, light inner frame of steel or iron girders, designers could construct very tall buildings that were also relatively light. Today's skyscrapers also incorporate a light inner frame of steel girders to hold up the entire building.

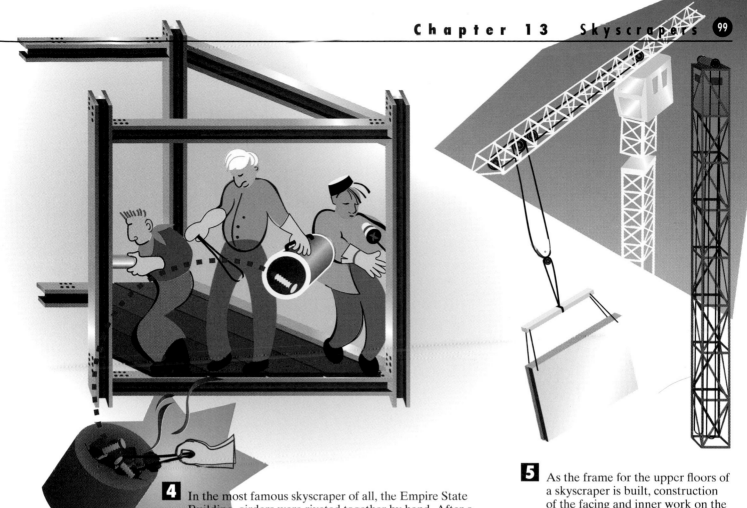

4 In the most famous skyscraper of all, the Empire State Building, girders were riveted together by hand. After a steel beam was lowered into place by a crane and temporarily bolted, a riveting crew made a permanent connection. The heater in the crew heated rivets in a forge until they were red hot. With tongs, the heater tossed the rivet to the catcher, who caught it in a bucket and rammed it into a hole. The bucker-up held the rivet in place with a heavy steel bar, while the driver used a compressed-air hammer to pound the rivet into a cap, holding the beam in place.

5 As the frame for the upper floors of a skyscraper is built, construction of the facing and inner work on the floors below is proceeding. So, while the frame for the top of the skyscraper may still not be finished, floors below may be almost complete. Derricks, cranes, and freight elevators in the partially finished building carry building materials and workers to the upper floors while the lower floors are being worked upon.

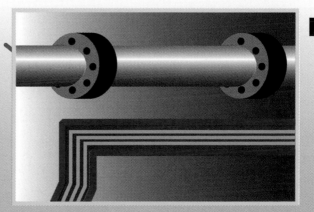

6 When a portion of the skyscraper's frame is complete, construction begins on its outer walls. Depending on the design, the walls can be built from a variety of materials. For example, one of the earliest and most elegant of skyscrapers—New York City's Woolworth building, completed in 1913—is covered in terra-cotta. First, approximately 16 million bricks were placed around the building's steel framework. Then, terra-cotta bricks were connected to the bricks and cemented in place.

7 The electric wires, water pipes, heating vents, telephone wires, elevators, and other utilities are installed on the lower floors while the top of the skyscraper is being constructed—as are the building's inner walls.

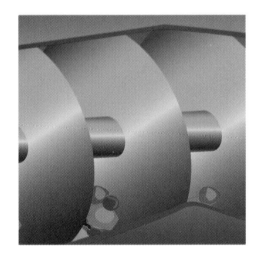

CHAPTER

14

Tunnels

S NAKING UNDERGROUND THROUGH many cities are a variety of tunnels. Some tunnels allow trains or subways to travel; others are built for cars. Tunnels traverse rivers, bays, and oceans, and sometimes are built so that expressways can travel underground to avoid disrupting city life above.

Tunnels used for transportation have a long history. The first known tunnel was built by the Romans in 36 B.C. in Naples, and was nearly a mile long.

While many traffic tunnels are relatively short—the width of a river or bay, for example—some are quite long. The St. Gotthard tunnel in Switzerland, for example, is a 10-mile tunnel for cars. And the Seikan tunnel in Japan, a railroad tunnel that connects the islands of Hokkaido and Honshu, is nearly 33 miles long. And probably the world's most famous tunnel—called the Eurotunnel, the Chunnel, or the Channel Tunnel—connects England and France underneath the English Channel. The Channel Tunnel is 32.2 miles long.

Tunnels are built in several different ways. Some, such as the tunnel now being constructed beneath Boston Harbor to connect Boston with Logan Airport and outlying cities and suburbs, are sunken tube tunnels. In this type of construction, huge sections of metal tunnel are built in a factory. Both ends of each section are sealed watertight. The sections are towed out through the water and then sunk to the bottom. Then divers bolt the sections together. Inside, the sections are welded together and the seals are cut away to make a long, continuous tunnel.

Other tunnels, such as the Channel Tunnel, are instead bored through rock and soil. A tunnel boring machine (TBM) does the work. It has a huge head, with hard tungsten cutting rollers and teeth, that eats through rock and soil. The rock and soil are carried away by conveyor belts and carts. As the tunnel is built, cladding, or lining, is put on it, and then the insides are finished.

The construction of the Channel Tunnel, which made use of technology such as lasers to guide the TBM, is the culmination of a long-held dream to link England and France. The first plan was proposed as far back as 1802; carriages pulled by horses would have rumbled through a brick passageway under the English Channel.

How Tunnels Are Built

How tunnels are built depends upon the length and size of the tunnel and the kind of soil and rock through which the tunnel will be built. In many cases—when the material to be tunneled through is softer than bedrock but firm enough that it won't collapse, for example—a tunnel boring machine (TBM) is used. A TBM was used to dig through the seabed beneath the English Channel to build the Eurotunnel.

1 The front of a TBM is essentially a giant drill with teeth and cutting rollers that cuts through rock and soil. Some TBMs can bore more than 400 feet of tunnel in a single day. The TBM used for the Eurotunnel had more than 100 cutting rollers and 200 teeth, and rotated at a rate of two to three times per minute.

2 Hydraulic jacks push the cutting head of the TBM forward through rock and soil. In the Eurotunnel, the jacks were guided by laser beams so that the tunnel could be bored accurately.

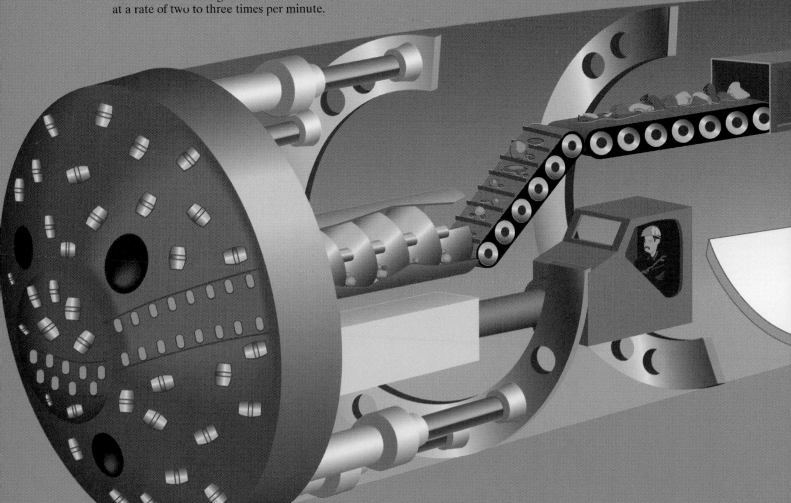

5 During construction, the tunnel must be ventilated to provide fresh air and carry away any gases that might build up. Pipes carry in fresh air and carry out stale air and gases.

3 The soil and rock carved by the cutting head of the TBM is passed to a conveyor belt, which hauls the waste away. In the Eurotunnel, for every three feet of tunnel drilled, 2,472 cubic feet of waste had to be carried away.

6 When the cladding is in place, work begins on the utilities, pumps, roadbeds or rails, and anything else that will be within the tunnel.

4 As a tunnel is bored by a TBM, it must be lined so that it doesn't collapse. This lining is called cladding. The cladding is often built of metal or concrete. Cladding is passed into the tunnel in sections, and is carried by conveyor belts, carts, or other heavy equipment. Cladding can also be made in the tunnel itself. The sections of the cladding are so huge that they are lifted into place by machines. Concrete is used to seal the sections of cladding and to make the tunnel watertight.

How Sunken Tube Tunnels Are Built

One common method of building tunnels under water is to bury massive metal tubes in the seabed. The San Francisco Bay Area Rapid Transit (BART) system's tunnel under the San Francisco bay was built this way. It is composed of two almost four-mile-long tunnels approximately 130 feet below the surface of the bay.

1 A series of huge metal tubes, watertight at each end, is built in a factory. These tubes will eventually be welded together.

2 A massive trench is dug in the seabed or riverbed where the tubes will be placed.

3 Heavy-duty barges tow the metal tubes into position over the trench. The tubes are then lowered into place.

4 Diving crews swim to the tubes that have been placed in the trenches. Using special equipment, they bolt the outsides of the tubes together. To ensure that the tubes stay in place and remain waterproof, they seal the tube's joints.

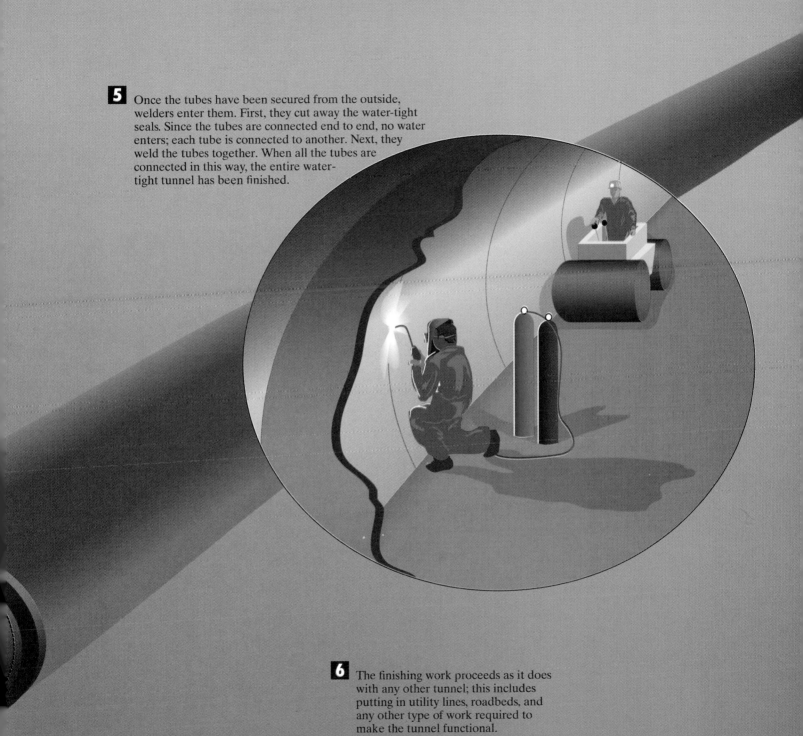

5 Once the tubes have been secured from the outside, welders enter them. First, they cut away the water-tight seals. Since the tubes are connected end to end, no water enters; each tube is connected to another. Next, they weld the tubes together. When all the tubes are connected in this way, the entire water-tight tunnel has been finished.

6 The finishing work proceeds as it does with any other tunnel; this includes putting in utility lines, roadbeds, and any other type of work required to make the tunnel functional.

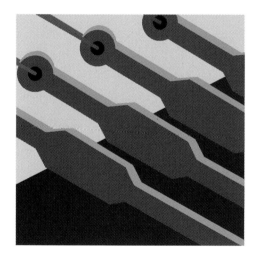

CHAPTER 15

Bridges

A BRIDGE CAN BE as simple as a log laid across a small stream or as complex as a massive steel-cable suspension bridge spanning a gorge. Bridges are among the most common and inspiring sights in the city, and at times they are valued as much for their form as their functionality—witness New York's Brooklyn Bridge or San Francisco's Golden Gate Bridge.

In general, there are three main types of bridges: beam, arch, and suspension. A *beam bridge* is possibly the most common type. This bridge is held up by abutments at both ends and often also by piers along the bridge's length. An *arch bridge* is held up by one or more arches. A *suspension bridge* has metal cables suspended from main cables along the length of the bridge to hold it up.

Bridges have been around for as long as people needed to cross rivers. One of the most famous of ancient bridges was the Old London Bridge, an arched bridge that took 33 years to erect, finally being finished in 1209. The more famous arched London Bridge (which was taken apart and moved piece by piece to Arizona, where it now resides) was completed in 1831.

There was a problem with many bridges built before the Industrial Revolution. Since they were built of heavy material such as stone, if they became too large they could literally collapse under their own weight. The development of cast iron changed all that. Its strength and relatively light weight allowed much larger bridges to be built more safely then ever before. The Ironbridge, an arch bridge made of cast iron rails and finished in 1781 in Coalbrookdale, England, spanned the Severn River and showed the possibilities of this new technology.

Suspension bridges are among the most dramatic and majestic of structures. Notable examples include the George Washington Bridge and the Golden Gate Bridge. Suspension bridges were at first rather small, simple affairs, but by the mid-nineteenth century much larger ones were built. Britain's Saltash railway bridge, finished in 1856, was held up by suspension cables hung from massive wrought-iron tubes more than 16 feet in diameter.

By this century, suspension bridges became the world's longest and most majestic bridges. New York City's George Washington Bridge became the world's longest bridge in 1931, at 3,500 feet, and the Golden Gate Bridge bested it in 1937, at 4,200 feet. As the following pages will show, these bridges are impressive not only for how they look, but for how they were built as well.

How Suspension Bridges Are Built

Suspension bridges are among the most common—and most beautiful—of bridges. In a suspension bridge, thick metal cables are strung from towers or piers, and suspension cables hanging from these main cables hold up the deck of the bridge.

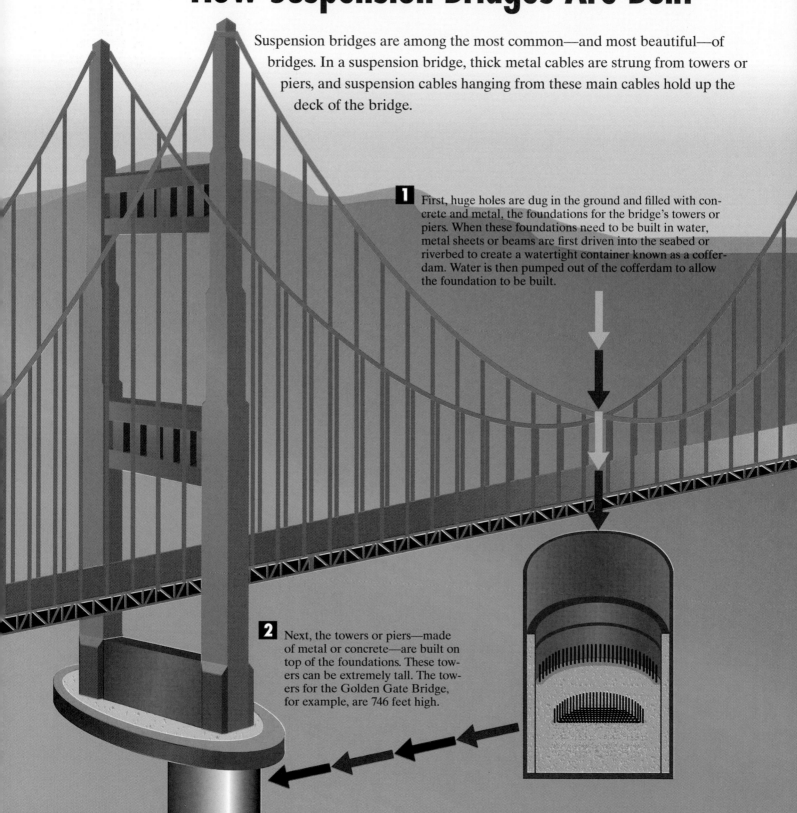

1 First, huge holes are dug in the ground and filled with concrete and metal, the foundations for the bridge's towers or piers. When these foundations need to be built in water, metal sheets or beams are first driven into the seabed or riverbed to create a watertight container known as a cofferdam. Water is then pumped out of the cofferdam to allow the foundation to be built.

2 Next, the towers or piers—made of metal or concrete—are built on top of the foundations. These towers can be extremely tall. The towers for the Golden Gate Bridge, for example, are 746 feet high.

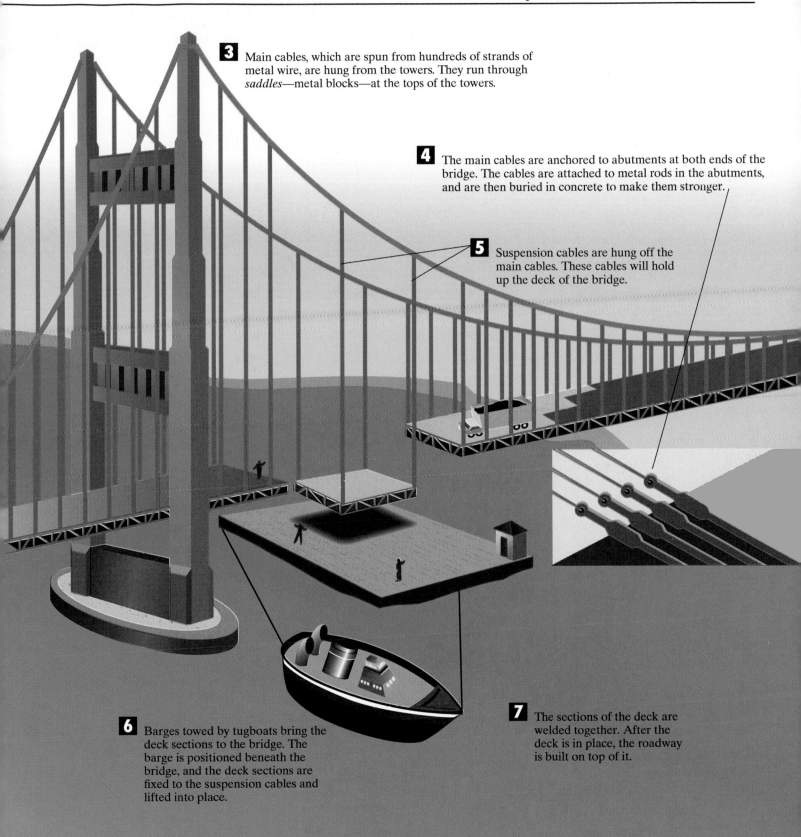

3 Main cables, which are spun from hundreds of strands of metal wire, are hung from the towers. They run through *saddles*—metal blocks—at the tops of the towers.

4 The main cables are anchored to abutments at both ends of the bridge. The cables are attached to metal rods in the abutments, and are then buried in concrete to make them stronger.

5 Suspension cables are hung off the main cables. These cables will hold up the deck of the bridge.

6 Barges towed by tugboats bring the deck sections to the bridge. The barge is positioned beneath the bridge, and the deck sections are fixed to the suspension cables and lifted into place.

7 The sections of the deck are welded together. After the deck is in place, the roadway is built on top of it.

Moving Machines: Transportation in the City

4

CONTENTS

F YOU ASKED most people living or working in the city what their most annoying daily problem is, getting into and around the city would most likely be at the top of the list. Traffic jams, delayed buses, trains, and subway cars—all take their toll on the quality of urban life.

The truth is, though, that it's surprising how efficiently people are moved through the city. Consider the millions of people who make the daily trek downtown and the number of miles they travel in the city itself, and it may seem miraculous that anyone gets anywhere at all.

What makes all this possible are two types of transportation: the automobile, and public transportation such as subways, buses, and trains. For the hundreds of years before the 1950s and the 1960s, public transportation was king; people didn't drive into and out of the city every day because most people already lived in the city and took public transportation to work. As far back as 1832, horse-drawn streetcars appeared on the streets of New York City. Then the industrial revolution hit and steam locomotives appeared, shuttling people between and within cities. In the 1880s, the electric streetcar made its appearance, and soon after that the underground electric subway was born; the first subway in the United States was built in Boston in 1897. Subways, electric trams, and trains became ubiquitous in American cities; above many city streets were suspended the electric cables that powered the public street cars. In fact, in Brooklyn, New York, so many electric trolleys crowded the streets that it gave rise to the name of a local baseball team—the Dodgers—because the locals were always dodging street cars.

With the advent of cheap gasoline, automobiles became ubiquitous in the 1950s and the 1960s, allowing the suburbs to bloom rapidly. While people often still use public transportation to travel within cities, most people live outside of the city and drive their car into work, giving birth to that most dreaded part of the urban day—rush hour. The automobile became the victim of its own success, and now the daily commute, instead of being a convenience, has became something of a nightmarish necessity for many, and for some people it can take hours out of their day.

In this part of the book, we'll take a look at transportation in the city. We'll see how subways work, and take a look at automobile-related technology, such as smart highways.

In Chapter 16, we'll see how subways work. Subways are referred to as *heavy mass transit*, since they can carry up to 60,000 people per hour on a single track. *Light rail transit*—such as electric street cars—can carry only from 5,000 to 15,000 people per hour on a

OVERVIEW

track. We'll look at how electricity powers a subway system, which in many ways has remained unchanged since it was first developed around the turn of the century.

Chapter 17 takes a look at the automobile in the city. We'll take a look at what are referred to as *smart highways*—highways with built-in intelligence so that they prevent gridlock and make the daily commute more bearable for all. These smart highways are only now being built, and their designers hope that they can undo much of the damage done by automobiles by reducing commuting time and therefore cutting down pollution—and in the process make a better quality of life for all.

How Subways Work

WITHOUT SUBWAYS, cable cars, and streetcars, the modern city couldn't exist. It would not be possible to move the millions of people through and below city streets without this effective means of mass transportation.

Even before motors there were streetcars. As far back as 1832, teams of horses pulled the first streetcars down New York City streets. Soon steam power and electricity were used to move people in and out of cities. The world's first subway system, the Metropolitan Railway, opened in London in 1863. It differed from modern subways in one very important respect: Steam locomotives, not electric power, provided the muscle to move people. It soon became clear that electric power was more efficient than steam in powering mass transit. A forerunner of electric streetcars was running in New York City in 1874, and by 1888, in Richmond, Virginia, the modern electric street railway was born. The first underground subway in the United States was built in Boston in 1897. Just seven years later, in 1904, New York City followed suit and never looked back, constructing the largest subway system in the world.

Subways are often referred to as heavy mass transit, because they can transport tens of thousands of people an hour—up to 60,000, in fact—on a single track. They can do this because many cars can be hooked to a single engine, and because they can travel at high speeds underground—there is no need to slow down for traffic. Light rail transit (LRT), such as electric street trains, can only transport from 5,000 to 15,000 people per hour on a single track because they can pull fewer cars and because they need to slow down for traffic.

Subway systems and other forms of mass transit began to go out of style in the 1950s and 60s, as the automobile became the vehicle of choice for many Americans. However, in later decades, subways, LRT, and other forms of mass public transportation experienced something of a rebirth.

For many people, hurtling into the darkness beneath the ground with tunnel lights flashing by remains the formative experience for moving about in the city. While commuters may not always enjoy the ride, it's often easier than sitting in heavy traffic for hours. And one need only look at the pleasure a young child takes in riding the subway to be reminded again that these trains are not merely about moving large numbers of people about with the greatest efficiency—the subways are part of a city's mystique as well.

How a Subway System Works

Subways run on electricity instead of on fuel. Electricity is sent to the subway train via the third rail, which is commonly off to one side of the two main rails, although it can instead be located in the middle of the rails. This third rail usually carries between 500 and 700 volts of electricity.

A conducting shoe—also called a pickup shoe—on the bottom of the train conducts the electricity from the rail to the subway's engine, and also powers its lights, doors, and heating and air-conditioning systems. Beneath the third rail is an insulator, which ensures that electricity doesn't leak from the third rail.

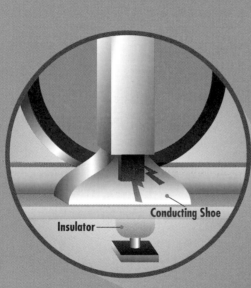

Insulator

Conducting Shoe

Third rail

Main rail

Electricity needs to complete a circuit in order to keep continually flowing. In a subway train, after the electricity is conducted to the motor, it flows back through the train's axles and then onto the main rails. From here, it flows back to the generating station or other source of power.

Some subway trains can travel above ground on streets as well as below ground in tunnels. When they travel above ground on streets, trains get electricity from an overhead electric line, which is much safer than an exposed third rail. Electricity is transmitted to the train's motor by either a wheeled or sliding shoe contact, or else by a collapsible pantograph system (pictured here). Trains that travel above ground in this way are called light rail transit (LRT). Some buses and trolleys are electric powered, and they also get their electricity from overhead wires.

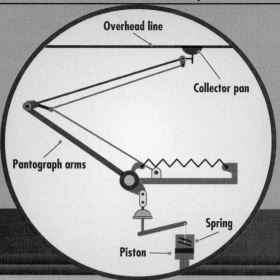

Overhead line

Collector pan

Pantograph arms

Spring

Piston

Subway trains are commonly controlled by a lever. When the conductor presses the lever, it moves the train; the more the lever is pushed forward, the faster the train travels. When the lever is moved back, the train comes to a stop.

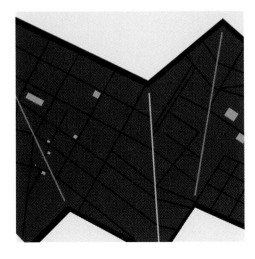

CHAPTER
17

Beyond Gridlock: How Smart Cars and Smart Highways Work

THINK OF THE two words that are perhaps the most frustrating part of life for anyone who works in a city. Didn't take you that long to find them, did it? Rush hour. Morning and evening drive times have become something that no one enjoys but everyone must endure.

Los Angeles freeway tie-ups are legendary; New York City is well known for traffic gridlock. But these monumental traffic snarls plague just about every city in the country, not just its two largest.

Traffic jams do more than merely frustrate millions of people each day—they take environmental and economic tolls as well. Air pollution is much worse because of the millions of cars stalled in traffic every morning and evening. And one estimate holds that traffic congestion causes $100 billion in lost productivity in the United States every year.

A growing number of people believe that the way to help solve our country's traffic problems is by building *smart highways*, also known as *intelligent vehicle highway systems* or *IVHSs*. These smart highways would use sophisticated computer and communications technology, sensors embedded in and suspended above highways, and even satellites orbiting the earth to help ease traffic jams and route traffic more efficiently. Information about traffic would constantly be routed to a central bank of computers that would automatically adjust traffic flow when situations warranted it. The timing of traffic lights would change, alerts would flash to drivers, and onboard computers in cars would automatically tell drivers to avoid tie-ups ahead and take the proper alternate route.

Cars would get smarter as well—they would contain onboard computer systems capable of planning and displaying the best driving routes, depending upon the current traffic and driving conditions.

These systems may sound futuristic, but in fact, they are already being used, and they are the subject of an enormous amount of research, including pilot programs in the United States and across the world. Los Angeles, New York City, Chicago, England, Japan…the list of pilot projects is long. In the United States, an industry group has been formed to promote smart highways, and local, state, and federal governments are pouring significant research dollars into them as well. You may have already driven on a smart highway and not realized it. In the coming years, increasing numbers of us will begin to reap their benefits.

There's no doubt that smart highways and smart cars can't solve our traffic congestion by themselves. But they undoubtedly will help, and as anyone who's ever been stuck in a morning commute knows, a little help can go a long way.

How a Smart Highway Works

Traffic congestion, especially during rush hours, may be alleviated through the use of smart highways, known as intelligent vehicle highway systems or IVHSs. Smart highways are an assemblage of technologies that will work together to make highways safer and less congested, primarily through automatically sensing traffic problems and patterns and rerouting traffic as needed.

1 In one system now being used, digitized video cameras are placed at traffic lights. These cameras detect whether cars are in motion or are stopped at the light. The cameras relay this information to a powerful microprocessor that interprets it and then adjusts the length of the red and green lights to ensure a smooth traffic flow.

Sensor

2 In a more comprehensive approach to smart highways, sensors are used along highways throughout an entire region to measure traffic flow and speed. Infrared sensors can be hung from bridges or traffic signs, or placed along the sides of the road. As cars pass through the sensors' infrared beams, the number of cars and the speed of the cars are recorded electronically.

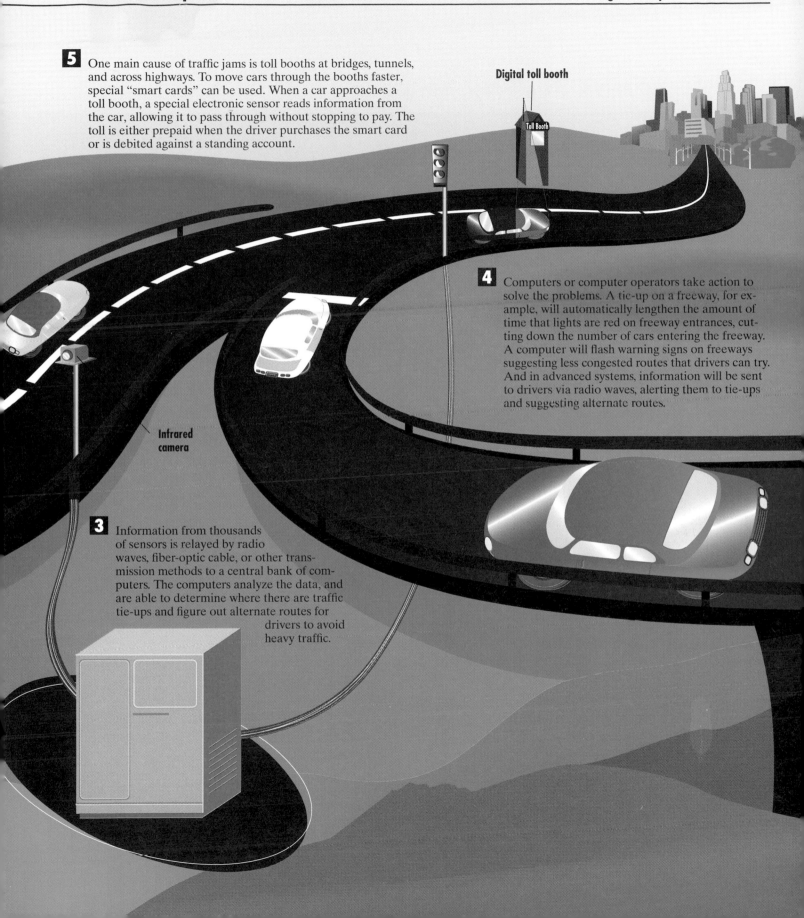

5 One main cause of traffic jams is toll booths at bridges, tunnels, and across highways. To move cars through the booths faster, special "smart cards" can be used. When a car approaches a toll booth, a special electronic sensor reads information from the car, allowing it to pass through without stopping to pay. The toll is either prepaid when the driver purchases the smart card or is debited against a standing account.

Digital toll booth

Toll Booth

4 Computers or computer operators take action to solve the problems. A tie-up on a freeway, for example, will automatically lengthen the amount of time that lights are red on freeway entrances, cutting down the number of cars entering the freeway. A computer will flash warning signs on freeways suggesting less congested routes that drivers can try. And in advanced systems, information will be sent to drivers via radio waves, alerting them to tie-ups and suggesting alternate routes.

Infrared camera

3 Information from thousands of sensors is relayed by radio waves, fiber-optic cable, or other transmission methods to a central bank of computers. The computers analyze the data, and are able to determine where there are traffic tie-ups and figure out alternate routes for drivers to avoid heavy traffic.

How a Smart Car Works

A number of test programs have begun that take the concept of smart highways a step further—smart cars. Smart cars have built into them computer and communications equipment that guide drivers to the quickest way to their destinations, based on the current driving and road conditions.

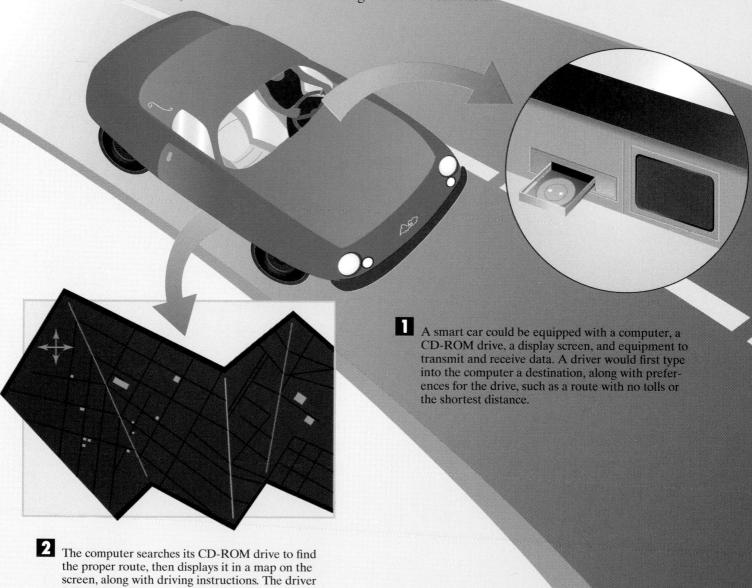

1 A smart car could be equipped with a computer, a CD-ROM drive, a display screen, and equipment to transmit and receive data. A driver would first type into the computer a destination, along with preferences for the drive, such as a route with no tolls or the shortest distance.

2 The computer searches its CD-ROM drive to find the proper route, then displays it in a map on the screen, along with driving instructions. The driver follows the route.

3 As the car is being driven, the computer transmits information about its destination and current location to a satellite. If at any time during the trip traffic congestion slows down the car, that information is transmitted via radio to a central traffic information center. The traffic information center uses that information and other traffic data gathered from traffic sensors to determine where there are traffic tie-ups and other problems.

4 The traffic information center automatically sends alerts to the computers of drivers heading into congested areas, warning of traffic problems and suggesting alternate routes.